Post Cards
From Another Gospel

Dave & Harold,

A self-published product of what
I believe the Lord had on my
heart. I hope it changes you
in your walk; in God's Word !
Hope you are all well !

God's Grace to you,

Love,

Bry   Jn-14:6

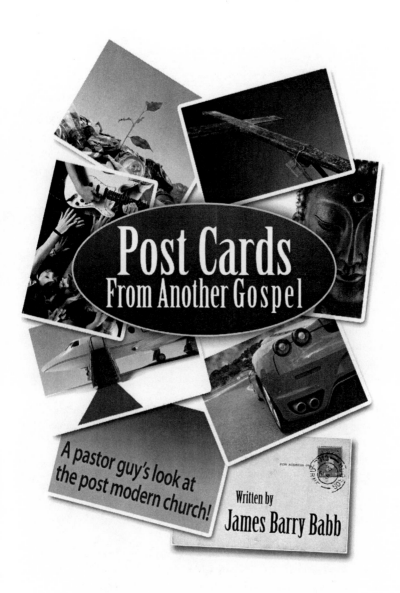

Post Cards
From Another Gospel

A pastor guy's look at the post modern church!

Written by
James Barry Babb

WinePressPublishing
Great Books, Defined.

WinePress Publishing (PO Box 428, Enumclaw, WA 98022) functions only as book publisher. As such, the ultimate design, content, editorial accuracy, and views expressed or implied in this work are those of the author.

Unless otherwise noted, all Scriptures are taken from the *New King James Version*, © 1979, 1980, 1982 by Thomas Nelson, Inc., Publishers. Used by permission.

Scripture references marked NIV are taken from the *Holy Bible, New International Version®, NIV®*. Copyright © 1973, 1978, 1984 by Biblica, Inc.™ Used by permission of Zondervan. All rights reserved worldwide. www.zondervan.com

ISBN 13: 978-1-4141-1802-4
ISBN 10: 1-4141-1802-3
Library of Congress Catalog Card Number: 2010905843

Contents

Acknowledgments vii

Postmodern Hymn #915 ix

Introduction. xi

Postcards R Us 1
Postmodernism Defined: When Pigs Fly! 11
"Another Gospel". 27
The Utter Irrelevance of Cultural Relevance. 47
Seeker Ye First the Kingdom of Felt Needs 63
Elvis Is Out in the Shack Listening to Miles Davis 77
Twenty-Somethings Just for You;
    Social Justice Under Review 95
A Postcard from the Hangar:
    The King Air 200 Is Blowin' Oil! 111
Mr. and Mrs. Decision-maker, Come on Down! 125

The Full-color Travel Brochure. 141
Repentance: A Treasury of Grace 155
Postcard Postscript: Lunch Under the Bamboo Gods!. . . . 167

Notes 173

Acknowledgments

I AM VERY grateful for the loving support of Camille, Lori, and Brian—my peeps! You remind me every day how I have been lavished with God's love and favor and how profound is the description of *grace* as that which is undeserved.

Russ Porcella, senior pastor at New Covenant Fellowship in Knoxville, Tennessee: You invited me to join with you and that amazing congregation to minister for eight incredible years! You remain a mentor and a friend whose life of personal integrity and faithfulness to God is something I draw upon every day.

Steve and Carla McRee, my dear friends and co-laborers at Shepherd's Gate in Livermore, California: Your commitment to take the broken lives of abused, addicted, and homeless women and their children and to provide a place for the love and power of God through the Holy Spirit to save, heal, and bring hope is a model for showing the world who Jesus is! Your lives show that reality as well.

Mike Coupe, director of The Place of Hope and pastor of Nashville Recovery Church, my dear brother who is faithful to the call of God on his life to minister to the homeless, addicted, and hopeless of the streets of Nashville and Middle Tennessee with the power of the gospel: Your encouragement to me is priceless, and I love ministering with you!

Jim Oxendine of GoToNations and John Cope, founder of Making Jesus Famous Ministries, my friends and big brothers in the Lord: Your timely words of encouragement over the past twenty years have been a provision from God. I am grateful for your friendship, your counsel, and the fact that you both make me laugh.

Allen Basham, pastor and dear friend: Your patience with me and your prayers through the early years of my walk with God are a priceless treasure. Your tireless intercession and love for me for these thirty-two years demonstrate the provision of God for a friend who sticks closer than a brother.

Postmodern Hymn #915

They say all paths lead to the same destination
I hear them say—all colors bleed into one stream
Your truth; my truth; like belly buttons—everybody's got one
No need to preach absolutes, you see—O how we love the mystery!

Truth claims—mind games—deconstruct—we're all out of luck!
My felt needs—trump old creeds—orthodoxy, dry as a bone.
Sensitive seekers with easy-bake preachers—
"How do I keep my grass green?"—gospel message left the scene!
(Just like Elvis, dressed in velvet—they done left the building).
Toleration—celebration—let's make it clear—we don't want no
    rigid dogma here!
Proclamation—abdication—next thing you know, you got—*no
    gospel nation!*

Sunday morning set the mood—indie band has found the groove
Pastors' stylin' real smart—macchiatos served in the dark
Eccu-meni-cal man—social justice is my plan—and that's about as
    doctrinaire,
Unless of course, you wanna talk—*Clean Air*—then I'm downright
    expository.
Wanna know the Greek for carbon footprint?

Regener-a-tion, justification—that's way too much theology—one
    more cup of mystery, please! And this time, without foam—
    would you?
It's *not* important what you know—but we're thrilled, Mr. Seeker,
    that you made the show
You see, creedal postures much overrated—truth has
    always been overstated.
Anyhow—isn't mystery more *fun*—than having that truth *gun*—
    pointed at every*one's* head?
How you ever gonna build community that way? Huh?

You see, we will not offend you—we got only "good news."
Stumbling blocks are "old school"—feeling bad just isn't cool—
Cuz we remove the scandal—now it's safe to handle
Sin, judgment, and the cross—are golden oldies—not for us.
How 'bout "*another gospel*" serving? And Elvis has still left the
    building!
Or maybe took the candle-lit path to the café.
Another hit of that culture coffee, please.

Now here's the honest truth—the only thing we're sure of
You're okay; I'm okay—everybody's got their way, so who are you
    to judge—Uhmmm?
"I ain't no naked and poor—don't call me no naked and poor."
God loves me just the way I am! I ain't no naked and poor man
I ain't no naked and poor. Am I? Nahh!

Introduction

IT WAS A Tuesday evening in late September 2007, and I was cruising the religious programming on the satellite channels. I came across a program called *Answers in Genesis*. It was so good that it made me realize how bad the rest of "Christian TV" is. That very night I swore off Christian TV for a while—except to keep watching *Answers in Genesis*.

A few months after that night, while violating my own self-imposed sanction, in the span of not more than a week, I saw three separate broadcasts where three preachers were parked on exotic beaches selling vitamins, anti-aging creams, and prosperity tapes. I couldn't believe it! But there they were, poolside, hawking their wares. All that was missing was the theme from the *Love Boat* taking them to commercial breaks, featuring these same preachers selling other products and services. I wondered, *Who's actually buying this stuff?* But I digress.

The ministry of *Answers in Genesis* does fantastic work educating Christians on the imperative of believing the literal Creation account as opposed to *millions of years* of evolution. Little did I know that stopping and listening to that one television program would begin a two-and-a-half-year process culminating in my writing a book about postmodernism and the church.

How did I get here? Well, it took moving across the country, spending a whole lot more time than I thought in finding what's next for me, and receiving lots of encouragement from those around me. Somewhere between the place of seeking God and being unsure of having anything of particular interest to say, I felt a release to write down what had been marinating inside me for over two years. What resulted is *Postcards from Another Gospel: A Pastor Guy's Look at the Postmodern Church*.

Right at the outset, I would like to tell you why I have written this book. In twenty-five years of ministry, eighteen of them as a pastor, I have come to the place where my observations and experiences have compelled me to look at the church and her relationship within the postmodern culture. I have always been a curious and conscious observer of the culture, cognizant and interested in trends, people, and the events that shape our set of values and social practices. I studied history and philosophy as an undergraduate, and have always been interested in cultural and historical perspectives of our society. I have also had some level of involvement in many of the church movements and trends I write about in this book.

The era of postmodernism presents very profound challenges to the church, for we are in a time when objective truth claims are met with suspicion and skepticism. Universal truth is being replaced by a preference for *interpretive* truth, where society puts a much higher premium on *me* and my subjective experience while placing less emphasis upon former universal beliefs about what is true and false. This is the very essence of postmodernism. I wrote this book (a diary of sorts) as if you and I were in an elevator and I had one minute to answer your question, "What is postmodernism and how has the church been affected by it?" Now I'm not sure one needs to spend a whole lot of time preparing for such a contingency, but nevertheless, I volunteered for the job.

I wanted to get a "primer" in your hands so you can begin recognizing worrying cultural trends. As you will readily see, my writing is not in the nature of an empirically based research thesis. Rather, it is part personal journey and part informed observation developed over many years. I do not seek to trace postmodernism's origins or deeply develop its philosophical, theological, or academic constructs. But I recognize that the postmodern church is here and doing a booming business. There is much debate on the antecedents of postmodernism. Many feel it derived from a synthesis of Descartes's rationalism with the British empiricist's view of "If it can't be handled or observed, then it can't be true."

And what about the current attacks on the truth claims of Christianity? Have they gained postmodern currency from such purveyors as Marx, Nietzsche, Freud, and others who overtly and forcibly asserted the particular deconstruction of religious truth claims? These are great foundational questions, and there are many books out there to help answer those important questions.

This is not one of them. Instead, it is a book applying the perspective of postmodernism with very troubling aspects of some church movements and cultural trends. Put in another way, this book is a "street level" conversation about postmodernism and the church.

I have tried carefully not to be offensive. I am compelled, however, to say that more and more in the context of church we are hard-pressed to find contemporary meaning and application in the words of Jesus, who assured us that "If anyone desires to come after Me, let him deny himself and take up his cross and follow me" (Matt. 16:24). In its stead, we have trumpeted an "easy evangelism" and a belief that temporal pursuit and fulfillment is just as important to God as the sanctification of the Holy Spirit that allows us to truly glorify him in the earth.

Postcards from Another Gospel is a call for Christians to reverse this humanistic, self-absorbed venture, and return to the historical and powerful truth claims of the Bible. The culture literally is dying for it! This is the same culture that the church has way too often mirrored instead of led.

Truth and Repentance

What motivated me to write about all this? Two words: *truth* and *repentance*. Let's start with the former. My wife, Camille, and I became instantly drawn to watching *Answers in Genesis* every Tuesday evening. In the course of a very short span of time our entire family was greatly touched by that ministry. We began ordering their DVDs, and we were even able to attend a conference that Ken Ham, the director of the ministry, held in northern California.

The Answers in Genesis ministry caused me and my family to rethink much of what we believed regarding creation and evolution. I always fancied myself a believer who was "broad minded" enough to allow for a little flexibility. I did not like being associated with "rigid" or "dogmatic" Christians. I never did subscribe to macro evolution (which results in larger and more complex changes over time) as it relates to humans. I always landed on the default position that even if humans did evolve in any more general way than natural selection within a species, God was the initiator. That at least allowed me to reconcile my ignorance and unbelief, which at the time I arrogantly mistook for my brilliance and tolerance, as demonstrated in my total deference to secular science on the subject.

But in the spring of 2008, I began changing my mind completely. The Holy Spirit allowed me to see how I had compromised my faith and my belief in God's Word. The more I learned about the importance of not compromising the truth claims of the Bible, the more I was granted the grace to repent. My mind changed on the subject.

Once I was able to see and fully accept the truths of Genesis, I developed a zeal for that truth, as the staff at Shepherd's Gate—a ministry to homeless women and their children (where I was the pastor) will attest. Bless their hearts! As I wanted to communicate everything I was absorbing, they became my guinea pigs in many staff Bible studies. If I got a new DVD, it was not long before they got to see it. Whatever truths I was learning, they got the unfiltered version. It was an amazing time. I had no hesitation teaching, preaching, or otherwise talking to anyone about the Bible and creation theology. I still don't.

While staying rooted in the incredible theology of the book of Genesis, I began to broaden that interest out to Christian apologetics, which is the defense of Christianity, in general. This is something I had done throughout twenty-five years in ministry, but my interest became especially keen during this time.

The following summer I began reading and listening to lectures by Ravi Zacharias, R. C. Sproul, Frank Turek, and Albert Mohler. These men are amazing in their knowledge, resolve, and ability to defend the Christian faith. I also began rediscovering the wisdom of Francis Schaeffer, whose teaching on Christianity and culture, now thirty years old, was prophetic in describing our present situation.

I was particularly drawn to Ravi Zacharias's lectures on the existence and identification of God. This opened up an entire wellspring of fresh desire within me to look at the God of the Bible in a way I had never done before. This was a sovereign work of the Holy Spirit, because spending countless hours researching, handwriting notes on a dozen legal pads, and listening to teaching on who God is, was not something I would normally have been prone to do for hours at a time over six months.

Something else was very different as well. I was beginning to get more insight on the need for proclaiming the truth about

God, humanity, and the role of Christianity in a postmodern culture. The more I listened and read, the more I got the sense that it was not going to be sufficient just to know how to defend the faith. Of more importance is *communicating and proclaiming* our faith and the truths of Scripture to this culture. The reason is clear: It is the gospel that changes the culture.

In September of 2008 I went to Web sites featuring Ray Comfort and Todd Friel, where they referenced an evangelist and preacher named Paul Washer. I had never heard of Washer before, so I looked him up on the Internet. I accessed archives of his messages, and while listening to Paul Washer, I came upon John Piper. Then for me everything changed. God had suddenly and profoundly brought the culmination of the entire previous year's study into focus, and that focus took the form of a single word: *repentance*.

I listened to the preaching of Paul Washer and my heart would be smashed into pieces. In thirty years as a believer, I had never experienced such a feeling and awareness of conviction, sorrow, and release. Almost continuously from September until March my heart groaned and ached for my sin against God. During those times when I didn't think it was possible to go any deeper, the floodgates of sorrow would open up again and again. And for those six months, the focus of repentance was almost exclusively on my sin against God. A couple of months into this season, I would ask the Lord, *who do I need to go to*, he would affirm over and over, "me." The Holy Spirit did bring people to my awareness when all this was going on; God has been very gracious in those transactions as well.

The Holy Spirit showed me that I had too casually approached God and that I had been arrogant and irreverent in not seeing him for who he is—the Holy One. I had taken the Lord and the Scriptures for granted, lost my zeal for God's presence, and developed an unholy affection for the temporal things that had bound me. And all the while I was preaching freedom to everyone else. I became convicted regarding my view of the cross, and my ascent to shallow, lukewarm evangelism, with its man-centered emphasis and methodology. I was also confronted with a pathetic resignation I had carried for seventeen years as a pastor—that since I was not an evangelist, preaching a gospel message with any regularity was something for someone else to do. My view of my calling as a pastor was self-focused and shallow, and I was ashamed of myself. I had become just "the worship pastor" and the "counseling pastor." The reality of these sinful misconceptions and self-deceptions continued to flood my awareness. What is a pastor fundamentally if not a proclaimer of the gospel of Christ? Even though a pastor may not have the gift of evangelism, his first cause, so to speak, should be in communicating the good news, should it not? Otherwise, I should go sell shoes. Or worse yet, stay on as a hireling.

Yet at the same time, even when I thought I could hardly bear any more, I sensed more grace, freedom, and love from God than at any other time in my walk as a believer. To be clear, I have treasured the mission trips, the times of revival and renewal, and seeing the miraculous power of the Holy Spirit in healing, deliverance, and restoration in the lives of people. However, *never* have I experienced more grace and more of the presence of God than during that six months. God lovingly allowed me the grace to go to deep levels of sorrow. My mind had truly been changed because my blackened heart was being dealt with. The real truth of the gospel began to really matter!

Repentance is the primary treasure of all the gold of my experience as a Christian. It is the posture I have asked God to make resident in me for all my days. God's kindness and patience and love brought me to the place of brokenness and submission. It was, and is, an unmitigated act of divine goodness, when I deserved nothing of the sort. I was fully aware of that imbalance of justice, which made me all the more grateful for what was happening to me. It is my prayer that it remains an unfinished work of grace.

Supernatural Empowerment Found in Repentance

It was difficult during that time to wrap words around what I was experiencing. I sensed that I was not to talk about it, but rather embrace it and let it set my life on a course of a fresh pursuit of God.

When I would try talking about it to close ministry friends, I would raise more questions than answers in their minds. I would only screw up their understanding; I didn't have a clear enough distance to properly put in perspective what was going on. So I learned. Finally, one pastor friend looked at me and asked if I was basically disavowing my previous thirty years of experience in the Lord. That was when I finally got a clue and quit talking about it. I just didn't know how to communicate it…yet. It would be akin to kissing your spouse passionately, while trying to assess how well you are executing the kiss. You can't do both at the same time.

I began pouring my energies into God's Word. I spent three months alternating between the New Testament book of Romans and Martin Luther's *Preface to Romans*. I was able to see why John Wesley, upon reading this book, was "strangely warmed." I then turned to the writings of George Whitefield and Jonathan Edwards, whom I had studied a decade earlier when our church was sovereignly touched by the Toronto renewal, a great world-wide outpouring in the mid-nineties. Edwards' *Distinguishing Marks of a Work of the Spirit* was one of the doctrinal works that helped bring a historical and biblical explanation to what was happening with aspects of the renewal outpouring. The sermons and writings of these men, along with C. H. Spurgeon, have been priceless resources to me.

Never before had I had such an unquenchable desire for God's Word and for proclaiming its timeless truths. I began reexamining the doctrines of our faith, including justification, sanctification, and substitutionary atonement. They began to really matter. I will refer to the historical doctrines of the church many times in this book because unless believers under the leading of the Holy Spirit learn and treasure the historic doctrines of the faith, the gospel message will be muted. If a Christian does not know how they are justified (or made right), they are ripe for legalistic, self-righteous pursuits. They may also be ripe for theological error and outright heresy. I am convinced with all my heart that repentance is the key for the church to return to her calling of proclaiming truth to the postmodern culture. And in that proclamation, the attending doctrinal truths will be as water to a thirsty person. They are no longer the dogmatic yokes around my neck as I used to fear. They are pillars of a great foundation that are sources of great joy for me.

My affiliation as a Christian for all these thirty-plus years has been more or less in streams of the independent charismatic church or with Vineyard Association churches. After I was converted, I received the baptism in the Holy Spirit. I fully embrace the grace that Martyn Lloyd-Jones calls an "encounter" in the Holy Spirit that empowers Christians in their faith and their daily living, and that is a separate grace from salvation of the believer.

From a historical perspective, if one considers how the church grew in its first couple of centuries, it was through the clear proclamation of the gospel, followed by persecution and signs and wonders of the Holy Spirit practiced in the lives of new Christians. However, I have no quarrel with those who believe the spiritual gifts are not active in the present age (they are called cessationists) because I believe that what binds us is the commonality of our salvation and not the exercise of any spiritual gift. I just don't believe that the Church in the first, second and subsequent centuries got the memo that the Holy Spirit was toning it down. I have witnessed the healing, deliverance, miracles, and the prophetic reality of the Holy Spirit far too much and in far too many places in the world not to believe His present-day ministry is still relevant. The Spirit and the Spirit alone is able to infuse the supernatural empowerment of the Lord to the believer for his sovereign purposes. The ultimate proof of the presence of God's Spirit is whether these experiences provide an abiding fruit in the lives of people—for that is the genuine and ongoing work of the Holy Spirit. The evidence I have seen of spiritual power in the lives of people has been overwhelming. That is not to say that everything that comes down the pike is of the Holy Spirit. Not by a long shot.

Accommodating the Culture

Though I am convinced by the Scriptures of the Holy Spirit's present-day ministry, I find myself in alignment, in part, with similar thoughts of Lloyd Jones on the matter. That such empowerment by the Holy Spirit is from above, from the pleasure of His will, and *comes down* to equip the believer to testify of Jesus. This simple truth desperately needs to be re-embraced. Such a grace is not primarily *Christian-centered*, as in an ancillary possession that identifies me, and that I claim as my own, as some spiritual accessory. And as it relates specifically to gifts, the Spirit's distribution of gifts is *Christ-centered, always* pointing to; indeed always testifying Christ… Jesus. Tongues by the way, although an important and effective gift, are not a hill that I die on. The Bible gives a narrow employment of its use both in intercessory prayer and corporately (publically), with specificity that prescribes a minimal utilization and directive for interpretation. There's been far too much emphasis on tongues from both inside the Charismatic movement (from over-emphasis and extra-biblical excess), and outside the Charismatic movement (from hypercriticism and outright condemnation). I also believe Scripture teaches that those who are born again have the Holy Spirit. There is no other requirement. The Holy Spirit distributes gifts as he decides according to the will of God. If one has the gift of tongues, fine. If one does not, that is fine too. The Holy Spirit sanctifies both. The fruit produced in the believer is the evidence of God's work. The apostle Paul tells us to "eagerly desire the best gifts" (1 Cor. 12:31).

I am indebted to God for the great preaching and teaching I have benefited from. The Holy Spirit has used the messages of people like Paul Washer, John Piper, John MacArthur, Mark Kielar, Ray Comfort, Todd Friel, and Mark Driscoll as a gateway to what he continues to work in me—an abiding hope and faith in God and his Word.

I have continued to be very blessed over the years by Bill Johnson, Dutch Sheets, Mike Bickle, and Lou Engle, who through *The Call* is prophetically and passionately calling this nation and the church to repentance. Every time I have participated in one of Lou's events, I have come away with a sense that there are very few true prophets in America who live their lives in a singular devotion to God while grieving for the sins of a nation and crying out for that nation to repent. Lou Engle is such a man.

I was involved in the early 1980s with the Word of Faith movement, which emphasizes confessing verses found in the Bible. The idea is to confess what the Word of God says and then you will receive what it is that you confess. For the first two or three years as a new Christian, I identified with that stream of thinking. Specifically, I was an advocate of the prosperity gospel and subscribed to its "name it and claim it" doctrine. It taught that God always provides material prosperity for his children. To me at that time it sounded great! I had no idea that God's will for me was to walk in divine health and wealth all the time. After a few more years of Bible study and walking in faith with him, I concluded he does not—not at the expense of being conformed to his will. What God wants is for me to die to self and stay hidden in him, knowing he is my Redeemer and my Provider and that *his* purposes will define me and give meaning to my life.

During the early 1990s, when I entered ministry full time, I became a strong proponent of what is called the "seeker sensitive" church model. The Seeker Sensitive movement aims at making church services so relevant and so appealing that the whole world wants to be there. I felt that if the church could just be relevant and refine her message that we could attract unbelievers on a spiritual journey and try to fill up his or her "god hole." It made sense that if we presented ourselves as a church that was not so rigid we could get a whole lot further with the culture, especially if we also met their practical and relational needs while showing the love of Jesus. After we gained their trust, I thought, we could then preach the gospel to them. It all sounded reasonable to me. But I began changing my mind as the church where I was on staff, in a sovereign move of God, "un-seekered" my theology through a sustained move of the Holy Spirit in our midst.

In the late 1990s and into the mid 2000s, I became intrigued by yet another church movement—the Emergent movement. This was sort of like the Seeker movement, but on steroids. It was different in that they had a grasp on the whole postmodern philosophy. I thought their approach to seeking authenticity in worship and community was a breath of fresh air, and I still believe that. Their passion for the arts and all things cultural seemed like a very attractive model for a postmodern world.

The Emergents were and are successful at capturing the angst of the age—the skepticism and doubt that has come to define the postmodern era—while then disarming the culture by presenting a church model that recognizes and reinforces many of the concerns of the postmodern culture at large.

As I look back upon all these models over the last thirty years, I am struck that there is some truth in all of them. In other words, there is a biblical basis for some of what is done in the postmodern church.

Therein lies the problem.

What God has impressed upon me during my own thirty-year journey, culminating in the last two-and-a-half years with *Postcards from Another Gospel*, is that much of the postmodern church has accommodated the culture by *becoming* an expression of the culture, complete with deconstructing and deemphasizing historical biblical claims. This has been accomplished instead of being a force for countering and then reshaping the culture. And our proclamation of faith as defined in the institution of the church is seemingly more and more muted in substance and effect.

Postmodernism is not necessarily easy to define. As I previously said, my desire is to write this book in a way that would be very accessible to the reader. With the exception of chapter 10, *Postcards from Another Gospel* is a light but not lightweight read. I want readers to come away with a simple understanding of some of the tenets of the time in which we live. And I want readers to be able to see that fidelity to God's Word through the proclamation of the true gospel is the only way to bring distinction and clarity to what is otherwise fuzzy and blurry. My desire is for you to be able to examine your own life as a believer in light of where you are in the culture by looking at what you believe. Is it grounded in the truth claims of the Word of God? Or are your beliefs an integration of cultural reinterpretation of the Bible? Does it even matter as long as we are just doing the best we can?

If you do not think this is a worthy pursuit, ask yourself these questions: How invested are you in the notion that you should not judge or that you must be tolerant to all points of view? Does historical biblical doctrine really matter? Is it accurate for people to call themselves "Christian" so long as they assert that believing in something higher than themselves is sufficient? Do all spiritual roads lead to the same destination?

Postcards from Another Gospel is a call to the church to reestablish and stand upon biblical truth. That starts with an examination of what we are proclaiming to the culture. Is it the true gospel?

I hope you enjoy the read, and I hope you find it interesting and informative. More than anything, however, I hope you come away with a sense of renewed purpose for the pursuit of the truth of God's Word and the resolve to take your place as a believer to speak to this culture in your area of influence. I want to encourage my readers to proclaim the transcendent truths of the Bible. There is not much that is new in this book; this is just another installment, my version, as it were, of what many very prominent writers, preachers, teachers, and leaders throughout the Christian community have been warning about and encouraging for years.

I wish to shed light upon some of the trends, doctrines, and specific church emphases within Christianity that are troubling. As I have indicated, I formerly embraced many of them. I am not mad at anybody (well, maybe a little at those three preachers on the beaches), and I have sought carefully not to throw "Bible bombs." While I do bring up a few doctrinal concerns in context, this is not meant to be a book that emphasizes nuanced doctrinal differences. Rather, it highlights larger issues related to the modern-day mission of the church.

In any event, welcome to *Postcards*! I sincerely hope you will be enlightened, blessed, and inspired to embrace the fullness of your calling as a proclaimer of the truth—whether you are a minister, a congregant, a believer looking for a church, or someone who is not sure about their relationship with God.

Have a good read!

Postcards R Us

Anyone who has seen me has seen the Father.
—Jesus Christ, the Gospel of John

AFTER ALL THE brochure browsing and postcard images of lush beaches with fifty-foot palms and fresh fruit floating on top of infinity-edge pools, we finally landed in Kona, Hawaii, for our much-anticipated first excursion to the Big Island paradise. My wife was on a business trip to the island, and my son and I stole away, courtesy of frequent flyer miles that we actually got to use, which in and of itself was no small miracle.

We began with the twenty-or-so-mile drive north from the airport to the beach resort, which was one of only four resorts on this stretch of the western coast of the island. As we started out on the drive, the first thing I noticed was that the terrain was primarily lava rock, largely treeless, with muted gray ground cover that wound upland into hills and mountain crags of mostly barren rock.

It was like nothing I had ever seen, and it certainly wasn't on the postcards. It was a strangely beautiful terrain that left me

1

trying to come up with an accurate description. I kept coming back to this eerie hybrid between what I picture would be the surface of the moon and the vast uplands from the coast of Scotland.

Because I can be susceptible to hallucinations on only fifteen minutes of sleep on a dawn flight, while tucked away in a middle seat, I could have sworn that on one stretch of the road a large open flatbed truck passed us and I saw the strangest thing. In the back of the truck was Neil Armstrong in a spacesuit, with a golf club, chasing Mel Gibson, who was donning a kilt and yelling, "Freeeeedom!" With that disclosure, my wife immediately insisted I put down the macadamia nuts and take a catnap.

As we got closer to the resort area, we were all struck by this amazing contrast as we looked to the left and saw plush green areas that looked as though they had been carved out of this barren terrain. They frankly looked almost out of place and artificial, as if planned. They definitely did not fit the overall flow of the terrain. Yet, as we entered into the lovely self-contained resort, the whole place seemed transformed into the postcard image that had been so attractive.

Oh, yeah—I found out from the bellman on the way to the suite that the green areas were in fact planned, trucked in, and basically assembled on site at the resort. All the things that went into making this exquisite scene were like terrestrial ingredients in some giant resort recipe. You just mixed it all with seawater, and the next thing you knew, you had instant Blue Hawaii… Elvis!

Nevertheless, it was a beautiful place and we had an incredible week, down to snorkeling in the artificial reef that had just been dredged and installed under the new ownership. I didn't think I would ever get pumped about seeing a four-foot carp being curious about my toes, but I must say it was quite a daring adventure in three feet of water.

Typically one gets postcards from a friend or family member, and it is usually such a warm occasion when that happens. You normally get a very flattering visual from the place where the card originates, provoking a delightful image of whatever happens to make that particular destination special. There is also this space for a handwritten note, which is kind of neat, especially in a time and technological age when handwritten *anything* is unusual. Twitter is great, but it's still not as quaint as a postcard. Well, I don't know…perhaps there is something romantic about captivating the interest and intrigue of five thousand people at one time to deliver vital information, such as you are signing off temporarily to pour Rid-X down the toilet so the septic tank doesn't back up into your kitchen sink. A postcard certainly cannot capture that kind of collective intrigue.

Furthermore, you may be like my wife, Camille, who collects postcards from every destination that she or we have been fortunate enough to visit. She finds great pleasure in rotating them on the fridge and securing them with magnets, which she also collects from every place we have ever visited. Ever. In our entire lives! I'm just saying…

A Small Snapshot Creates a Large Image

Looking at the magnets, I cannot believe we have actually visited so many places. We have magnets from countries I have never heard of, let alone visited. I don't remember ever going to Djibouti; I don't even know what continent it is on. Camille has to be buying these things out of somebody's attic on Craigslist or eBay.

I am also not privy to the calculus she employs when deciding the rotation of her postcards on the refrigerator, but throughout the year I can go to the fridge and be instantly transported (or violently drawn, if I happen to have any metal on me) to the gorgeous southwest coast of Ireland, the Elvis truck stop in Israel

3

(I live for that one), or the Monterey Peninsula in California, which, though it was only an hour or so from where we recently lived, nonetheless became one of our favorite places to visit.

The point is that a postcard is special because of its personal touch and transcendent ability to elicit imagery, fond memories, and pleasant sentiments, which is not to be confused at all with the characterization I would use to describe my emotions about refrigerator magnets. But the postcards themselves are inviting, while offering just enough visual or written information to form a mental portrait that has you longing to "be there" sharing some exotic destination with someone special or transfixing your mind and emotions to elicit a special memory if you have been fortunate enough to have visited there in the past.

A lovely and specially written postcard is proof that it takes only a small snapshot to create a large, lasting image. But that is really all a postcard is: a tiny snapshot. It may highlight the best of a place, yet it is incapable of revealing an accurate picture of the area or experience as a whole. Who would have thought that along a twenty-mile inland stretch of Kona, just a mile away from the beach, there was land that could have doubled as the set of *Braveheart*, or been a NASA training station for lunar modules to practice their touch-n-gos?

Or what about those exotic islands or coastal getaways in some country where, no more than one hundred yards inland from your resort paradise, there is wholesale squalor and abject poverty? Just outside your stucco-walled fortress, there can be quite a different scene, for sure! The story is repeated over and over at great destinations all over the world. This is one reason why more and more resorts are built and tailored to be "self-contained" or "all inclusive." They don't really want you to go outside the resort for the entire duration of your stay.

Yet many times when you do step out, you are likely to see segments of the local population begging on the street or trying to game you by selling a menial product or service, all in a variety of motivations that range from a con game to a daily effort for basic survival. You will often see overcrowding and inadequate transportation services, plus evidence of street filth, random crime, and extremely poor infrastructure. Not the kind of stuff that makes for a great postcard, eh?

Nevertheless, the shantytown is just as real and, arguably, more accurately depicts the defining reality of the destination as a whole—the beach resort only one hundred yards away notwithstanding. In a real sense, and certainly for the purposes of a vacation, you could argue that the two places are mutually exclusive. After all, you are here for only a week, and you do have the power to choose either-or.

I do not mean to lecture on the morality of choosing vacation spots, and I am not trying to sell timeshares. The point is that the postcard is going to take the recipient to one place or the other—not both. My trip to Kona is just a reminder to be aware that in a great many places both very different locations really do exist.

And know this: The best chocolate-covered macadamia nuts in the world are on that Hawaiian island!

Jesus and Postcards

Unlike the postcards described above, when it comes to Jesus and the gospel, we see the part as the sum of the whole. Jesus tells us in the gospel of John that "Anyone who has seen me has seen the Father" (14:9 NIV). So in Christ the image does not reflect a portion of what is real, but rather in him we see the true nature of how things really are—in its entirety.

There is no postcard version of the authentic Jesus or the kingdom of God, because the Father, the Son, and the Holy Spirit are unified in their authenticity and their message. The landscape of God's love is consistent, so that what would be revealed as a true image in any smaller likeness of him or his nature could not deviate nor be separate from what is revealed to be true of the entire landscape of his nature. Both the universe of God's love and the small places of his love are always consistently and faithfully interchangeable.

His postcard is the entire Book, from Genesis to Revelation. Any smaller image it projects comes, as in a postcard, from the same exact larger image, whose message is complete, consistent, and unchangeable.

I chose to include the term *postcards* in the title of this book in part to highlight both the nature and types of challenges to biblical truth in general and the message of the gospel in particular. These challenges to truth and sound teaching have evolved into contemporary assaults on the propositional truths of historic, orthodox Christianity and are the philosophical and cultural accepted byproducts of the postmodern accommodation that, sadly, finds a multitude of welcome mats across the spectrum of Christianity and the church.

So, the postcard in the title is a metaphor for the error, deception, and just plan complacency that have become all too commonplace in postmodern Christianity. Mind you, these errors are presented as exotic places, beach paradises, and warm sentiments because they are, after all, postcards. They emphasize in a very small space that which can only be imagined and presented as good. Unless, of course, you step outside of the image of paradise and into the full context of a church that finds much of itself in the throes of some very troubling aspects of postmodernism.

Some Postcards Redefine the Truth

The postcards sent to us by our postmodern culture are very enticing, but many times they are dangerous, because like most of what comprises false teaching, doctrinal error, and heresy, there may be the presence of some semblance of truth (an image) that is sufficient enough to draw one into the full web of deception and error. Or maybe the postcard may be sent as a not-so-subtle carrot, a novelty that attracts believers by distorting the meaning of passages of Scripture in order to accommodate an agenda that devalues both the person and the completed work of Jesus Christ and reframes those truths to present someone or something entirely different.

Perhaps the postcard is really not an invitation to overtly reject a biblical truth claim. Rather, it is a hearty approval of the dispositions of the heart that encourage us to follow a cultural mandate to create a god in our own image. In the old modernity this was called idolatry. In the postmodern world, this is called ... idolatry.

To be clear, I am not making the case in this book for or against issues that constitute longstanding debates within the church. This presentation is not intended to be another attempt to settle the historical and ongoing intra-church debates within Christianity, though I acknowledge their importance. I once heard R. C. Sproul, a theologian whom I deeply respect, refer to the important intra-church debates as "laborious" and "tiring but necessary so that truth does not get slaughtered in the street." I completely agree with that assessment. But those battles are not the subject of this book.

My intention is to distinguish the postcards that define (or redefine) truths that have been historically part of the main tenets of our faith regarding Jesus Christ, who he is, and the mission of his life and death. In other words, the things that determine whether or not someone spends eternity in heaven or hell, based upon their acceptance and beliefs regarding those tenets of faith. That is the kind of challenge we face today. It is a bit more fundamental in that I am talking about the promotion of postmodern views as distilled in much of the church that give rise to speculation as to whether or not there *actually is* a heaven or hell, as biblically defined.

As far as the internal debates go, I would sum it up this way: One can be equally convinced that both John Wesley, eighteenth-century Arminian, and Jonathan Edwards, eighteenth-century Calvinist, are glory-bound for eternity, not because they advocate and articulate brilliantly *different* views regarding this issue, but because they shared the unshakeable view of how salvation is gained by grace through faith in Jesus Christ.

It remains a daunting task to reveal the cultural proclivities blurring the lines between truth and "new truth," and determining whether the new truth is really an enlightened version of the old—or its complete contamination. When discussing wholesale cultural shift and its effects on so many things, it is all the more important for us to retain and promote the desire to communicate propositional truth in a language that can be understood and believed as either true or false. It is difficult because, among other reasons, truth is not always a clearly defined, black and white division.

Through the passage of time in the postmodern era, things formerly differentiated become wedded and meshed together, making it all the more important that the truth for the culture be applied with renewed vigor. It is the truth claims of the Bible that are not only relevant but uniquely equipped to bring into sharp focus the cultural lines that have been blurred.

I recognize that this is not a mutually exclusive endeavor and that it's not a realistic pursuit to somehow suggest we are able to pick and choose portions of the postmodern reality as if it were individual items on an all-you-can-eat buffet. Clearly, this is the era encompassing seamless cultural and societal undertones and patterns that have long since been successfully made mainstream, right under our noses. In many ways, the density of the trees of postmodern culture has impaired our ability to see the forest.

We cannot, however, compartmentalize the era in which we live. That is an impossible task while we are living in it. That kind of detachment would render us as lifeless as zombies. We cannot choose either the culture *or* Christianity because we are encultured Christians, alive at this time. Besides, in the end, Christianity is a faith and love relationship, not a detached sociological experiment. What we can do is elevate the value of proclaiming the truths of Scripture, which will draw very clear cultural distinctions while providing the true and only hope for the culture's salvation.

We must be diligent to measure all transactions in our lives by an *objective* standard of truth. For Christians, it is the objective claims and external truths of the Bible that matter most. And as such, they are completely sufficient to carry the day without nuance or reframing through the lens of such things as relevance, paradigm shifts, celebrations of esoteric mystery, or the marvel and virtue of liberation that comes from not knowing anything.

Postcards are quaint little pearls of thoughtfulness. They give us some idea of the tone of the place that makes it special or partly true. The postmodern church is sending them out in bulk, and it is going to take a real effort to discern what is true and what is not. But we have the standard of truth—the Word of God.

Welcome to the postmodern culture, church. Welcome to the church, postmodern culture. You have both grown up together. But let us hope that while inseparably in it, the church remembers that she is not of it.

Postmodernism Defined: When Pigs Fly!

I will know it when I see it!
Supreme Court Justice Potter Stewart on trying to explain
what constitutes a definition of obscenity.
—Jacobellis v. Ohio, 1964

OKAY, MR. AND Mrs. Leader, you are just about to conclude the biweekly Thursday night community group (formerly called a *home group* when we were still in the modern era) meeting, and, after taking the last prayer request, the host invites everyone to the kitchen for organic oatmeal cookies and green tea.

Just as everyone rises to move to the kitchen, a brand-new member of the church and first-time visitor to the group raises the following question: "Look, I know it's getting late, but I keep hearing about this and I just wanted to find out if anyone knows. May I ask someone, please—anyone—what is a simple definition of postmodernism?"

Everyone who can politely do so kicks it into another gear and races toward the kitchen in a mass exodus (disguised as a mass deferral to one another) with the exception of the leaders, who dash out in record time, declaring something about their babysitter texting and they have to go right away. What makes this particularly strange is that it's their own house they are leaving.

But three people are left, whose escape proved impossible because they were caught wedged behind the sectional couch and the wall. They were unable to find a quick route unless they had walked right past the visitor in indifference, which is not the kind of statement they wanted to make to their new group member. Instead, they settled for instant disdain for her in their hearts. Not wishing to appear rude, however, these three attempt to answer the visitor's question.

The first person to respond is Jill, who has been a Christian for three years and is a very faithful member of the group. "You know," she says, "I think it means the time we are living in now is past modern times and technology and stuff, and we are in postmodern times now—past all the modern things now, I think."

The visitor's look of moderate confusion is exceeded only by the utter confusion from the other two people standing next to Jill. Only now Jill finds herself sprinting to the kitchen in jubilation at a pace resembling someone who just got a positive ruling at a parole hearing. *I'm outta here!*

The second person is Matt, a twenty-something grad student who works part time at a coffee shop and has been a believer since he was eight (or twelve, he isn't sure). "You know," he says, "I'm not sure, but I think it has something to do with not being sure. You know?" He politely excuses himself, while managing to text three people on the way to the kitchen—two of whom were actually *in* the kitchen.

The third person is Don, who has been coming to the group for over a year and goes to church about two times per month. Don is very likable and has quickly established himself as everyone's favorite. Standing there, realizing the weight of the moment, and fully aware that he represents the last best hope for answering the question, Don responds: "Don't those cookies smell great? Seriously, I would just Google it, man. That's the way I find everything." With that, Don heads for the cookies.

The visitor thanks Don, but because of intolerance to oatmeal, she declines the invitation to the kitchen. Besides, it has already been a night of disappointment.

So, did anyone get it right? Did anyone get it wrong? Could all three answers be correct? Was anyone close in his or her response? How does the newcomer feel? Are there any more cookies left?

Such is the dilemma of defining postmodernism, an elusive quarry and a task that is difficult to accomplish through anything short of a doctoral thesis. And Lord knows, those are no fun to read. Even in the heroic pursuit of trying to "boil it down" you are likely to be required to contract the professional services of either Gandalf the White or a current board member from the Ayn Rand Society—or maybe one or more cast members from *The Matrix*—to give you any hope of a contextual understanding. (Even though I have seen *The Matrix* three times, I still don't get it.)

Furthermore, it is probably a safe bet that *Postmodernism for Idiots* will never be published, precisely because scaling down postmodernism to an identifiable set of tangible propositions, whether for idiots or valedictorians, is an equally impossible proposition. If it is true that all aspects of our society and culture are permeated with marks and evidences of postmodern influence, would it be a stretch to think someone could give us all a workable definition of what the heck we're supposed to be talking about?

What, Then, *Is* Postmodernism?

In the interest of both brevity and the prevention of the onset of a migraine, I will say that postmodernism is the era in which we find ourselves living that finds virtue in speculation and uncertainty as well as a moral imperative to reevaluate (deconstruct) previously held truth claims that the former modern era failed to give meaning to.

That modern era, with its *ideal* of reason and technological progress was supposed to bring meaning to life and validity to the individual, but somehow blew the opportunity and is now being replaced by the highly valued "subjective experience." In short, the gadgets didn't do it for *me,* so now let's make it *completely about me* without the pretense of technology, which didn't make *me* happy but to which I will cling anyway while sojourning my way through the twenty-first century.

In the meantime, *doubt* and *skepticism* are to be so present as to almost be celebrated in art, music, academia, philosophy, literature—in other words, the culture as a whole.

How's the head doing?

Fortunately, with the benefit of three Advil and the knowledge that the worst is now over, we can narrow the focus of our examination to one of its most identifiable yet troubling basic concepts. It is precisely this primary concept of postmodernism that is germane to much of the purpose for writing this book. So the difficulty of the task will, thank goodness, ease a bit, descending from the status of impossible to merely formidable.

This main concept is the postmodern view of *truth*—how it is defined and how orthodox Christian truth claims are under its all-out assault. I am not talking about an assault from the usual suspects of secular postmodern culture, for they are as predictable and transparent as ever. You know, Hollywood, the media, academia, art, and politics.

No, I am talking about an assault coming from within the institution of the church. The church? That's right, the church. This assault is propagated and given traction and credibility by Christians—and by those who perilously think themselves to be Christians, and almost certainly a contingency of false converts. And finally, the false teaching brought to you by…false teachers!

Crisis of Belief

Their proliferation is a natural cause and effect of the church culture, inasmuch as many of the precepts of postmodern thinking have become mainstreamed into the church. There is a crisis of belief in Christianity today. And no wonder. With the merger of postmodern thinking and a gradual generational decline in the proclamation and reinforcement of historical biblical truth, the vacuum that is created is quickly filled by willing vessels who trumpet truth deconstructions over orthodox Christian claims.

Things certainly seem to be turned upside down.

Not to despair, my brother or sister—not for one moment! Go ahead and worry a little, but don't despair. Because the net effect of this madness is that biblical truth increases the acuity of the contrast, making it ever sharper and its focus more and more keen. Otherwise, another explanation might kick in: We've all been dropped into *Alice in Wonderland*.

It is essential to see cultural transformation for what it is. The prevailing darkness of our time that fosters deceptions that would have us trade in the enduring merit and power of gospel truths for the shallowness of relevancy, has—by a stark contrast—presented us an opportunity, as crisis is bound to do. That opportunity is the unashamed proclamation of the good news of the gospel of Jesus Christ, stripped of its cultural baggage and diluted pretense designed to help it go down more easily, kind of like a bad medicine. In the culture that celebrates the deconstruction of truth in general, the truths of the Bible must be proclaimed all the more!

> Your truth…my truth—Like belly buttons
> Everybody's got one—No need to preach absolutes, you see;
> Oh how we love the mys-ter-y!
> Postmodern hymn #915

The Cliff's Notes version of the postmodern concept of truth is simply that truth is not universally true for everyone. It is a social construct that is interpreted differently from one group to the next and from one individual to the next.

Whither Objective Truth?

To say it another way, there is no such thing as universal, absolute truth. Or, as a nuanced position, all worldviews may equally lay claims to truth (even though they are not universally true).

I will repeat that for the benefit of those of you like me, who, after multiple viewings, still don't get *The Matrix.* Postmodernism *claims* there is no such thing as absolute objective truth. There are only subjective *claims* to truth, socially constructed, whose validity cannot be applied or transferred to the societal whole—not anymore. It is about the personal distilling of truth to fashion what's true for me and my group, and that its relevance be mine to own and mine to communicate. Or here is another way of putting it: Welcome to a normal morning on the set with the cast of *The View*!

In postmodern thinking, truth claims get reduced (deconstructed) to a vast assortment of colors painting the subjective evaluation of the experience. And that is the goal rather than a dogmatic claim of truth that is universally applied to everyone. That only messes up everybody's color canvas.

One more time now for clarity's sake: *Postmodernism says there is no such thing as absolute truth.* Just let the unmitigated irony, if not the contradiction, of that statement sink in. But secular postmodernists are not the only ones who think so. According to Barna research, Christians are equally split among those who believe there is absolute truth and those who *do not* believe there is absolute truth. This state of affairs absolutely should induce a four-alarm migraine.

Before you ask what postmoderns have been smoking, you may want to find out what they have been listening to in church the last few years. And if you think our truth problem exists only among a certain movement or type of churches, you would be wrong in that assumption. From Emergent to evangelical, from charismatic to Catholic, from seeker to mainline denominational, there is a crisis of truth in what is being preached and taught on what the Bible says about man, God, and eternal life.

Though this postmodern creed is self-contradicting—*in spades*—it is nevertheless a bedrock precept of postmodern thinking. How the contradiction is normalized remains a great mystery. Yet apparently the contradiction is being buoyed with the help of Christians who share this opinion of truth. How does a Christian who is affected by this cultural reinterpretation of truth not be affected in his view of truth claims that have been historically the foundation for the gospel?

For the postmodern mindset, anyone who does not toe the party line and has the audacity to continue claiming that objective truth can be known is guilty of marginalizing those who would disagree. That marginalization can lead to manipulation or even oppression, or so they say. To the postmodernist, a given societal truth is a *grand story* or *meta-narrative* that claims to dispense objective truth. It does so at the risk of snubbing those outside of the accepted claim or paradigm.

The big questions about life and the afterlife are, in the overall postmodern view, necessarily considered unanswerable and are therefore reduced to the status of being basically insignificant. In this perspective there are no provable transcendent truths from one time or culture to the next. What does get distilled as truth gets determined by individual communities of like-minded people who become bonded through shared values gained from their own individual experiences, or *stories*. Postmoderns believe we have all been sold a bill of goods for ages by a horde of cultural used-car salesmen. Now we better buy a warranty on everything that claims to be universally true, much in the same way prudence would require if we bought an '85 Yugo from Crazy Al's car lot.

Postmoderns are known more for what they don't profess to know than what they do profess to know. In some sort of postmodern, post-reasonable switch, a virtue is accredited on how well one can deconstruct things that are allegedly known. When you have reinterpreted it through your own lens, it becomes your own "story," which is to say, your own version of the truth. This is a centerpiece, for example, for much of the more liberal contingent of the Emergent movement, which we will look at more fully in another chapter.

Seeking to Emerge

This postmodern affirmation describes, in part, how some in the Emergent church movement view propositional truth. For many of our Emergent friends, the absence of concrete truths (what is known) gives way to a more virtuous pursuit of mystery (what is not known). I do not intend to critique the view of truth running through every stream that either represents or alleges to represent Christianity. Rather, my intention is to identify postmodern views of truth through a narrow lens that is reflected in churches and in Christian thinking.

Since the Emergent movement is predated by a cousin who went before them and blazed a trail, it is time to at least mention the Seeker Sensitive church movement within the narrow focus of truth claims. Originally available in only one size—mega—now seeker sensitive churches are available in a variety of sizes and venues in a city or town near you. It was the classic seeker sensitive model from thirty years ago that presently configures some of what Emergents took from their elder pioneers. At this point I am not sure which movement to thank.

As previously mentioned, the Emergents generally fall into lockstep with the postmodern view of objective truth. They have a negative disposition toward objective truth claims, except those that are interpreted in the context of community. This may, in some cases, bring into question some universally held claims of orthodox Christianity. On the other hand, their cousins who predate them, the classic seeker church, say they believe the historic orthodox truths. At least you hear many of them claim they do.

That's the good news.

The bad news is that much of their premise is built upon *not* actually telling anybody. At least not at first, and not directly. Certainly not the truths that have been determined to be politically incorrect.

The fear is that if people who venture through the front door of the church were told about such depressing things as sin, judgment, hell, and the need for repentance, they would not like it and they would not like the church for saying it. Soon they would be out the back door. Apparently the gospel needs to come in small doses, kind of like a hepatitis vaccine.

How much of an oversimplification or caricature have I just created of our emerging and seeking friends? Sadly, not very much of one. We will take a more detailed look later.

> Truth claims—Mind games;
> Deconstruct—we're all out of luck.
>
> Postmodern Hymn #915

We must not forget that in the postmodern view, objective truth claims are unacceptable because they can be manipulative, punitive, and exclusive. Truth is *individually determined*. Therefore, dogmatic claims are to be avoided since they cannot be applied across the board, and that is why everyone has his or her own lens (story).

It stands to reason that anything supporting such overbearing and narrow orthodoxy would not be held in high esteem. Such things as proof texts, doctrinal assertions, and various creedal postures are necessarily tools of suspicion at best—and instruments of oppression at worst.

Houston, We Have a Problem!

The potential dilemma on the horizon is that this postmodern mindset is speeding toward a head-on collision with the most fundamental assertion of the Bible, which is that Scripture's truth claims are, in fact, true—both objectively and transculturally. And many in the church today do not want to be "guilty by association" when the cultural thought police claim that Christians are too intolerant, judgmental, and exclusive. It presents a real problem, one that has the effect of silencing the message of the gospel. As Lutheran pastor Jerome Bruce surmises in *Proclaiming the Scandal*, it is one thing to speculate, surmise, or even believe for yourself, but to claim to *know* the truth and, worse yet, to actually be arrogant enough to proclaim that the truths are *for all* is intolerable. The result is that in the pulpit and among the congregants who sit in church every Sunday, there is created what Bruce calls a church that is "confessionally challenged." Our faith has become too uncomfortable to talk about. To quote the famous hero astronaut, Tom Hanks, "Houston, we have a problem!"

And here is the crux. Not only does Jesus Christ claim we can *know* what truth is according to his Word, he jettisons the problem to another galaxy by actually having the audacity to declare that *he* is objective truth. He said, "I am the way the truth and the life. No one comes to the Father except through Me" (John 14:6).

The importance of this contrast cannot be overstated; it is the theme that will be highlighted throughout much of the book. For *truth* is the crux of the entire matter. Our gospel message rests on the assurance of an objective, external, historical set of facts that form truth claims. It is *not* a subjective, experiential reframing of those facts but the *facts themselves* that validate their claims. Peter's sermon on Pentecost makes the point. In this amazing declaration, during one of the most profound experiential moments in Christianity, he attests to the historical Jesus with objective facts about who he is.

> Men of Israel, listen to this: Jesus of Nazareth was a man accredited by God to you by miracles, wonders and signs, which God did among you through him, as you yourselves know. This man was handed over to you by God's set purpose and foreknowledge; and you, with the help of wicked men, put him to death by nailing him to the cross. But God raised him from the dead, freeing him from the agony of death, because it was impossible for death to keep its hold on him.
> —Acts 2:22–24 NIV

It is the proclamation of these facts that is the pretext for his calling them to repent. And thousands do. Peter, in the midst of the Holy Ghost party at Pentecost, attests to the facts of the gospel so that the party did not become an end to itself.

Defining Moments

If postmoderns ever developed a motto regarding their view of objective truth, my guess is that it would read something as follows: "Truth itself, as a means of being true, is truly overrated." Outside of probably becoming the most popular bumper sticker ever at UC Berkeley, perhaps it would, by nature of its absurdity, remind the rest of us how important objective truths are. There are people who are mobilized by the sheer absurdity of slogans on bumper stickers. It happens all the time. When you get behind some Subaru on the Bay Bridge in traffic and you are forced to read "Whales are people too" plastered all over bumpers and back windshields, you will find that it often has an interesting effect on how you watch the news.

It happens this way. You find yourself sitting in your favorite chair, watching your favorite TV anchor reporting on a story from out at sea. You watch intently as the drama unfolds. You see three angry grad students, barely hanging on in a small motorboat playing chicken with a four hundred-foot whaling freighter in the middle of the Atlantic. There is only a remote possibility that the captain of the freighter is sympathetic to the protest and will veer off quickly and miss the tiny craft. Or not.

What you may be reluctant to admit to your spouse is that you are secretly pulling for the freighter anyway, even as you are screaming at those people to "get out of the way!" At least sometimes that is the effect it has on me.

The point is that times like these on the open sea can be defining moments. The utter contrast of truth and lies can provide very defining moments as well. In fact, I believe such a defining moment is upon us, and the meter is running. The postmodern culture has a problem with the certainty of truth outside of a very narrow subjective range. The angst from all that energy to deconstruct propositional truth is seen as a virtue, a celebrated notion that has little tolerance for truth claims in general, and therefore less tolerance for the historical truth claims of the Bible.

Words Are not Innocent Bystanders

And finally, within the postmodern world truth claims turn subjective and are culturally reframed because language itself is neither reliable nor adequate for communicating unbiased motives. Many postmodernists say that language keeps us *inside* far too deeply to step *outside* and be truly objective. Meaning and truth are, in part, language-framed. And there are no objective truths that can be known apart from communities that construct their truths from their language. It is as if universal truth is compartmentalized to groups as they develop and trust only their language. Universal transcendent truths are only as universal and transcendent as the small community determines.

Into an Ontotheological Oven—a god-Cake Rises

So why is the merger of relativism with the postmodern view of language problematic? Because it runs the risk of elevating you and I to the age-old position of defining God from our subjective criteria instead of receiving the external revelation of him, by him. The trouble is, he *IS* – transcendent and independent of our reasonings regarding him, and his revelation is both alien to us, and beyond our faculties to comprehend, let alone create. All must come from him to us – through his Word and by his Spirit.

Just as philosopher Rene Descartes had earlier implied, Ludwig Feuerbach later asserted that god's existence is preceded by my reasoning of him.[1] The fact that the bible claims God's pre-existent revelation to us actually trumps our ability to reason him into existence evidently remains subservient to age-old musings in many intellectual quarters. The 21st century postmodernist runs the risk of embracing a present-day rendition of a similar proposition—musings of human imaginings about God—in place of God's revelation, to us. This occurs as relative truth (subjective), as defined by an individual, is coupled with his/her context of language, thereby determining what is believed. Subsequently, any externally declared "truth" must be filtered through a relativistic and linguistic lens, creating for the postmodernist, a *truth du jour*, readily available to satisfy even the most finicky of interpretive appetites.

Moreover, postmodernists assert that words, as trans-cultural universal agents, are ineffective because they are inherently creations of personal prejudice. They are useful only for providing a social context and for reframing, while they carry the net effect of not actually meaning what they intend. Another way of saying it is that we are all just giving political speeches—and politicians enjoy an approval rating just slightly higher than sewer rats.

Let's use the former example of our astronaut hero to make the point. Astronaut Tom Hanks' famous words to the command center in Houston could not have possibly explained accurately what the crew and the ship of the Apollo flight were experiencing at that very defining moment on board the *Apollo 13* flight in 1970. For the postmodern, words can do only a minimal job of conveying information that is not somehow a tainted, improvable conclusion.

Hanks' words obviously were not referring to the difficulties and stress of impending doom from a variety of mechanical issues in the spacecraft. No. So he had to reframe the problem in terms of how words could be formed through his own subjective filters in order to convey his truth of the matter. It is anyone's guess what astronaut Tom was actually trying to communicate. Was he really trying to say something else other than the lights have all gone out, the oxygen is about spent, and we don't have any control over the controls? Or do you think NASA took him at his word?

Language is problematic for the postmodernist, and this is another reason to establish the notion that *truth must be held to be subjective and relative.* It is something left up to the individual or construct of the group to determine. In this perspective words are not innocent bystanders; they are vehicles to communicate hidden agendas and motives that could advantage one group over another.

If any of this sounds vaguely familiar, it should. In the late 1980s, before *postmodernism* became a household word and the term *codependency* was driving us all nuts from its grotesque overuse, this mode of postmodern thinking was evidenced in what was called *moral relativism, values clarification,* and *political correctness.* The only difference is that, through the passage of time, postmodernism has become more acceptable through familiarity, repetition, and tolerance, which creates the effect of inoculating the collective culture from the negative impact of its initial troubling characteristics.

As a result, postmodernism meshes passively and seamlessly into the fabric of our cultural and social institutions. As postmodern thinking is expressed in art, literature, academics, philosophy, music, architecture, and religion, it eventually becomes mainstreamed into the culture as a whole, while finally reaching the status of the accepted cultural norm.

This is all the more reason why believers must be diligent and must proactively contend for the standard of biblical truth—and not just to contend for it but to proclaim it.

For believers there is the necessity to swim upstream, to contend forcibly against the strong current of the destructive forces contributing to the demise of a culture. The moral imperative is there and it must be answered, especially if the culture promotes the deconstruction of truth claims that have historically helped define Christianity as the predominant redeeming value giver of our culture. Yet this is not unique to our time, nor does it present any more insurmountable obstacles now than it has in the past.

Viva la France!

We close this chapter with an illustration of the point. Some historians and philosophers note that the ten-year period that defined the French Revolution (1789–1799) qualifies as an era unto itself, or at least a unique subset of what was then the modern era. If the end of Napoleon's reign in 1815 is counted, the French Revolution lasted twenty-five years. It was so bizarre, with such complete social and cultural upheaval, that some scholars give it its own special historical designation. Historians also claim these years mark the official end to the eighteenth-century Age of Enlightenment. You think? I wonder if there has ever been a more understated assertion.

Because of both the ferocity and the velocity at which change completely redefined the French society, a chaotic transformation was ushered in at lightning speed. In short order, the country became a complete basket case.

Suppose you are living in Paris in 1795—halfway through the chaos—and every institution in the country has been turned upside down. Your entire culture is in the throes of a collective lobotomy because the arts, literature, politics, economics, philosophy, and religious institutions are all turned on their heads. Your nation's most prominent export has become exotic implements of torture forged and featured by the revolution. Robes Pierre has made cutting off heads with the guillotine the official national sport, while doing so with almost whimsical flair and complete indifference. Plus, during this time no one wants to go to Paris anymore, not even for the wine or the bakeries, because everyone is generally in a foul mood, not to mention there are no croissants left anyway. Now we know the situation is very serious!

Remember, it is just 1795, and you are only halfway through this national nightmare. There are at least five more years of this insanity yet to endure.

Is everybody in the country Looney Tunes? It might seem so, but there are people who are advocating truth and the reestablishment of order, some of whom even manage to keep their heads while so doing. Of course, they had to hide in the wine cellars when Napoleon seized control, even though he proved to be a slight improvement over both the whack job Robes Pierre and the unpopular Directory, the five people who held executive power in France whom Napoleon directly replaced in 1799. But then he abdicated control after not having a particularly good outing at Waterloo in 1815, and because it would be another century before booster seats and platform shoes would arrive on the scene, rendering the good general perpetually short both in stature and temper.

So the reasonable people assumed control and were on their way to establishing a parliamentary government to provide the steadiness that soon saw the cessation of the craziness. The fact was that everyone actually did not have a portable guillotine in his garage after all.

Eventually the French got to 1800; then 1815—finally! They did make it. The madness ended. Sanity was restored and France became … well … Perhaps we can look at another example, oui?

"Another Gospel"

*There's something in people that's spiritual, that's godlike.
I don't feel like doing things just because people say things,
but I also don't know if it's really better just not
to believe in anything either.*
—Angelina Jolie, September 2000

SO HOW IS that cultural Jesus working out for you? What about Jesus and his mission today? How is Jesus, the Son of God, likely to be presented in the postmodern secular culture?

In all too many circles, Jesus comes across as a much less threatening figure—a bit dumbed down and mellowed out. He is presented as a sort of passive fellow, in a Ghandi sort of way. A very cool guy with amazing morals, essentially nonjudgmental, and someone who doesn't especially want anything from me except that I be nice on my journey to find my happiness, which of course, the Lord wholeheartedly endorses. Come to think of it, many times I hear this kind of description by postmodern *Christians*.

He is a sage for the ages and is culturally relevant more because of his ethical standing and fine example of life application than for his divine claims. More and more our understanding of Jesus Christ is rooted in a cultural framework, featuring his humanity and speculations regarding where he lands on political and social issues. He is stripped of his status as the Christ and fashioned by his contemporary relevance instead of biblical Christology. And this Jesus really doesn't require anyone to worship him; he is more secure than that. Just believe in his ideal. The way his importance and influence in one's life is shown is by addressing the pressing issues of the day, and by treating others how we want to be treated, particularly the part on how we want to be treated.

And what of the contemporary mission of Jesus? Well, that could be anything from the impetus for a determined ecumenical effort of social justice to being a billboard or poster icon for human causes to create a planet with enough goodness that Jesus would actually want to come back to—in a figurative sense, of course.

How about the view of Jesus for many in the postmodern church? Unfortunately, see above. What about the view of his vocation? Ditto!

But above all, this Jesus would be formed *in my image*. After all, it is important to him how I feel and that I am happy and able to go through life without being judgmental toward people. Yep! That's the kind of god I want to serve. I wish there were two of those!

The Me(ity) Deity

Do you think I am over-generalizing? Maybe just a little. But let me ask you something: Have you ever heard of MTD? I'll give you a hint. It is not a car model by Mazda, neither is it a disease of the nose.

MTD stands for *Moralistic therapeutic deism*. It is a fancy term that came out of a large survey. Two authors conducted what they say is the largest survey *ever* of religious teens in America, covering over 3,200 interviewees in forty-five states across almost every identifiable religious stream in Christianity. There was also a small sample from the Jewish and Mormon faiths as well. The following is a summary of what this survey found that American religious teens believe.

God cares that they are *happy* and that they maintain their *self-esteem*. He is not particularly involved in their lives, except to solve their problems. Being *good* is important, as is *self-fulfillment*, unless being good gets in the way of their own self-fulfillment. In addition, being good is very important in going to heaven. Teens are inarticulate when it comes to their faith but *extremely articulate about their cultural interests*. For many teens, this survey represented the first examination and discussion of their faith with an adult.

Pass the Advil, please!

With this set of beliefs, our nation is ready for a lethal dose of heresy. I know we are ripe for a mass revival. That prospect is both very exciting when thinking about its onset, but very alarming when thinking of what happens in its absence. Since this was only a brief sketch of what this survey found, I encourage you to read it in its entirety by contacting the National Study of Youth and Religion, University of North Carolina, at youthandreligion@ unc.edu. But please—wait at least thirty minutes after eating.

It is now official: In the contemporary edition of Western Christianity, everything is about me! But this is nothing new. Men and women have been living by the creed of their own human-centeredness since the Garden of Eden. I just wanted to make the official announcement.

It is the same malady. It just gets reexpressed by whatever cultural vehicle happens to be on the timeline highway of history at any given point. However, if you add a couple of additional ingredients to the mix—unchecked materialistic access and excess, along with an unhealthy portion of entitlement—you get an especially lethal combination. It is humanism on steroids.

And humanism, or man-centeredness, is always a major precursor for seeds of "another gospel." After all, it just has to be about me! The true gospel is God-centered, which means it is primarily about God. The benefit I derive from living by it will not necessarily win me style points in the culture, but it will secure my eternity. That part is about me. Yet that important part makes me see the goodness of God. And the desire to glorify God with my life makes it all about him once again.

"Another gospel" is any other version of Christianity that adds to or subtracts from the true message of the Bible concerning the person and mission of Jesus Christ. But what about the Bible's claims of the exclusivity of God and, more to the point, its claims about Jesus? Specifically, what about his *exclusive* deity and His *exclusive* power to save us from the *exclusive* wrath of God in a horrifically awful and *exclusive* hell, which is the eternal residence for the unbeliever, *exclusively*?

The troubling thing is that these historically established, culturally transcendent truth claims are themselves under fire today for being ... too *exclusive*. That kind of exclusivity gets equated then with intolerance, judgmentalism, and arrogance. In other words, the garden variety, everyday cultural view of Christianity.

Now we are told we are not liked by people in the world because Christians give Christianity a bad name. And who can argue with that? And that could be said about any group with a population of more than one human being. But the fact is that if Oprah Winfrey were to assert the exclusivity of Christ, she would go from being a semi-divine cultural icon and great humanitarian to a has-been whose empire gets canceled. If she's lucky, she could get a job doing the 10:00 PM weather with WCOLD in Butte ... weekend edition!

30

Despite all the talk about how Christians mess up Christianity, it really is our *message* that is at the heart of the secular culture's disdain. It is all about the message, certain periods of the crusades and Captain Cook notwithstanding. So in an effort to swing the pendulum back to show how really cool and tolerant we are, many Christians may begin to overcompensate to a culture that is all too eager for us to change truth to a *version of the truth* that is hopefully more tolerable to culturally accepting ears. It is at this time that the prospect for error begins to worm through the hard drive to work its way to a full-blown virus of false teaching. The computer crashes, and no more YouTube. Where would we all be then?

Mephistopheles: An Odd Name for a Snake

The tendency to veer off doctrinal course is obviously not new to the postmodern church. This trend finds its beginning in the first three words in the book of Genesis: "In the beginning" in the Garden of Eden. Eve is there carrying on a conversation with Satan, while Adam was either on the couch watching *Sports Center* or, worse, passively observing the conversation his wife was having with the wriggling Serpent. We pick up the conversation in the third chapter of Genesis as Satan asks the woman, "Did God really say, "You must not eat from any tree in the garden?" (Gen. 3:1 NIV). At that moment, with that question, heresy was born. Or more accurately, heresy was hatched.

I once heard Ken Ham, president of Answers in Genesis, speak about this at a conference, and his message spurred me on to study his assertion and go a little deeper. Satan cunningly placed the bait for the couple in the arena of the trustworthiness of God's word, so that doubting what God says provides the opening and entrance into the entire deceptive transaction, making this event actually more significant than the final week of *American Idol.*

Did God really say? The answer is, God absolutely did say!

And herein lies the crux of the deception. Satan's goal was to set the table for humankind at the earliest possible moment in our existence to make us question the validity of the truth of God through raising questions about the sincerity of his words to the original couple. By asking Eve a question about what God had clearly already mandated, the Father of Lies launched a direct assault on the veracity of God, an assault triggering the entrance of sin and death into the world to all people who have since been born into an utterly fallen world.

But it also reveals the grand strategy by Satan to try to convince God's people not to believe his Word. It has to be the number one weapon in his arsenal because it is the one he pulled out of his hellhole first. And he scored a direct hit—right to the spiritual jugular of Adam and Eve, and, as a result, all their progeny.

There's Nothing New under the Sun

The Devil's strategy for today is deception, pure and simple. This is not an empirical sample, but I would bet a year's subscription to ESPN's *Game Plan* that if you asked a thousand Christians what was the number one strategy Satan uses to get at God's people, that would be the answer you would get. Following deception closely would be pleasure and pain. Yet we need to be clear regarding the distinction and nuance of the Enemy's deception.

Of course, the Devil and his angels want to promote lies to us about ourselves, our failures, and whether or not we are worthy of God's love. That's what prolific liars do, and Jesus said this was so of the Devil: "He was a murderer from the beginning, not holding to the truth, for there is no truth in him. When he lies, he speaks his native language, for he is a liar and the father of lies" (John 8:44 NIV). If anyone could win the liar's franchise, Satan could.

Yet let's be clear regarding the emphasis Satan makes when using his number one deception: *He is most interested in deceiving us into doubting the literal words, the Logos, of God.* After all, we are told in the first chapter of John's gospel that "In the beginning was the Word, and the Word was with God, and the Word was God (1:1 NIV). In fact, that entire passage is about God, Jesus, and the Word. In light of what we are talking about, this is an incredible passage. This whole word and language thing gives postmoderns a skin rash if anyone seriously relies on words to actually mean things.

For sure, the Devil did not come in with all guns blazing, making emphatic accusations about God being an overt and overbearing pathological liar. He reasoned with Eve in a pre-Socratic exchange that was softer and more palatable for her consideration.

The art of doubting was and is a carefully selected strategy used by the Enemy. And lest we find ourselves extolling the brilliance of Satan, remember that the Bible says it was more the art of the Devil's *cunning* that revealed Adam and Eve's vulnerability to disobedience. Since then, he has had thousands of years to be around humans. You would think that after the sheer volume of time even an idiot would find tendencies that could be probed in people. He is not a genius; he's just in it for the long haul.

Did God really say …? Creating doubt is the Devil's bull's-eye when it comes to targeting God's children. Doubt his Word and then you will doubt that he is who he says he is. And if he is not—then that leaves…me. If Satan is successful at deceiving me into not believing God's Word, then my bad day just got a whole lot worse because I have just affirmed a different gospel than what I first received.

By putting his deceptive spin on the Word of God, the Devil creates, in essence, an archetype of "another gospel." This is the lie that was proclaimed by Satan and received by Adam and Eve. Its ramifications for sin and humanity are far-reaching, and it becomes an insurmountable obstacle for us to overcome. It is in the DNA now. The sickness is sin, and it is terminal. Only faith in the resurrected Jesus Christ can defeat the inherent malady of sin.

After that time in the garden it was another few thousand years before the destruction wreaked by the consequences of sin would be utterly defeated—by the crucifixion and resurrection of Jesus.

However profound the garden sequence is, that is the record in the beginning only. The deadly subtleties that were transacted there can be seen in their full development by the time one looks ahead to the establishment of the church after the ascension of Jesus and the promise of the Holy Spirit had come to fruition at Pentecost.

The church had grown by phenomenal, supernatural leaps and bounds, with its message proclaimed in just about every direction of the known world. Everywhere that the Holy Spirit directed the apostles and disciples to go and preach, the gospel message was delivered in both certitude of doctrine and demonstration of power. And just as quickly as the gospel was established, the race was joined by the hordes of hell and their willing accomplices to pervert that very message. The church was simultaneously experiencing amazing growth while experiencing severe challenges to the message that was the primary vehicle for that growth.

Throughout the New Testament, but primarily in the books of Galatians, Colossians, 1 and 2 Timothy, 1 Peter, Jude, and 1 and 2 John, we get very clear insight into what the early church founders were dealing with. Remember, past is prologue and there is nothing new under the sun. This is a first-century version of our postmodern culture—one that finds a fertile ground for false teachers and false converts using age-old versions of humanism that feature the Me(ity) Deity.

IN HIS LETTER to the Galatians, Paul offers a stern warning as he speaks about the perils of turning from the true gospel for a different gospel (the Greek word *heteron* means another or a different kind). "I am astonished that you are so quickly deserting the one who called you by the grace of Christ and are turning to a different gospel" (1:6 NIV). He goes on to characterize the perpetrators as those who desire to "pervert" the message that was first preached: "Some people are throwing you into confusion and are trying to pervert the gospel of Christ. But even if we or an angel from heaven should preach a gospel other than the one we preached to you, let him be eternally condemned!" (Gal. 1:7–8 NIV).

Whether by adding to the prescribed and accepted doctrines, or, by introducing heretical error and false teachings altogether, there arose a plethora of different gospels in the early church.

The severity of the error is signaled by Paul's tone and the sharp words he uses to diagnose the disease that was afflicting the Galatians. He calls the believers foolish and confused and the heretics accursed. This was a very serious matter, and the manner in which Paul writes reflects such. If you were to say that today, it would get you a couple of years to life in the thought-police slammer.

WW(J)JD: What would Judaizers for Jesus Do?

The region of Galatia had many churches, and they were under a frontal attack from the Judaizers (legalists who taught that Old Testament laws were still binding upon Christians). The Judaizers did not deny that faith in Jesus was necessary, but they insisted that it was inadequate. To them, one must add to one's faith the observance of the Mosaic law, specifically circumcision.

That is not unlike today. One cannot just be nice and not judge anybody without having to add an affirmation for specific tenets of the cultural causes (law) of the day. In other words, in many postmodern church circles being a "true" Christian is not defined so much by proof texts and belief systems as by where you land on your "green" commitment—or other causes that the culture determines to be important in its orthodoxy. It is kind of ironic; I guess they have a kind of religion as well.

Yet we find Paul writing to the churches in Galatia because of gross heresy that had gained popular traction. He wrote to remind the Galatians about the truth of his gospel and how a person comes to salvation. All over the newly established church and in almost every missionary region, there was an attack from all quarters at the heart of the gospel message. Yet the response by the apostles is always *salvation by grace alone, through faith alone, in Jesus—alone.*

No place exemplified the intensity of this attack more than in the central region of Asia Minor. I have enjoyed studying this New Testament book (Colossians) for years because of what I believe to be its profound similarity with contemporary times. In Colossae, the true gospel was challenged by the active contingents of gnostics, Judaizers, occult practitioners, and a moderate-sized population of Jews. Believers here were combining aspects of these thought systems with other pagan and what we would now call New Age practices, including the worship of angels, into their faith. It was an old-fashioned New Age blowout! As a result, both the deity and the sufficiency of Jesus were being challenged.

One of the most troubling beliefs taking hold was the notion that Jesus was "semi-divine." In this time and place, he was one among many who were held in that view. Because of this status, it was believed by many that Jesus could not possibly meet all the needs of the Colossians and could not claim total authority in any matter. He probably could have sold a boatload of books on his speaking itinerary, but he could not claim complete and unique deity.

He was highly regarded, mind you, and even seen by some as very relevant and important, because, after all, he was semi-divine. He just did not rise to the level of the full expression of God. And add to that the belief that he certainly was not exclusively unique, according to the culture, for there were people like him floating all over the landscape.

Besides the belief that Jesus was semi-divine, there was another significant belief that held equal status. It was a widely held view that enlightened believers could achieve spiritual fullness through special knowledge and rigorous self-discipline, including special diets and other physical regimens. (Perhaps this would cause us to wonder if this was not the inspiration for the first sighting of a TV evangelist spending an entire telecast selling vitamins on the beach.) This belief is called Gnosticism. And if special knowledge, self-discipline, or special diets proved too stifling, then one would just turn 180 degrees to all-out hedonism, which was the other side of the same coin, but usually a whole lot more fun.

Self-actualizing in the Lycus Valley!

The Lycus River valley region primarily consisted of three towns: Colossae, Laodicea, and Hierapolis. It was a flourishing and prosperous area that had a special appeal to the well-to-do and the allegedly enlightened. The tri-cities were happening! Colossae, although starting to decline in significance, was the primary focal point, as it was from there that Epaphras, undoubtedly a pastor and influential church leader, was desperately enlisting the help of Paul to rein the church back in from the heresies that were becoming commonplace.

Laodicea, just a few miles away, was a city noted for its access to the finer things, including the pursuit of Greek enlightenment and gnostic gurus. But as noted later by Jesus in the third chapter of Revelation, the Laodicean church was lukewarm: "I know your deeds, that you are neither cold nor hot. I wish you were either one or the other! So, because you are lukewarm—neither hot nor cold—I am about to spit you out of my mouth" (3:15–16 NIV). You would not have wanted to drink the water there, but other than that, the city was buzzing.

Throw in the hot springs and expensive baths at Hierapolis, six miles down the road from Laodicea, where the rich and famous could be both spoiled *and* enlightened, and you have the makings of a thrilling first-century retreat and personal growth seminar that would rival any weekend with Deepak Chopra and Eckhart Tolle in Sedona.

The early believers were under tremendous pressure in the challenge of protecting their converts from the perils of doctrinal error and heresy from false teachers. The Greek philosophical and cultural influences, in all their expressions, were very formidable against the relatively young sect of Christianity. The tendency was to mix and match a little New Age with some Christian doctrine, a tad of law with a bit of body cleansing and dieting, some hanging out with angels, and private sessions with famous gurus. You know, just the normal stuff that marks any decent personal renaissance weekend.

In this region there was access to almost every known philosophy and occult practice imaginable and available in that part of the world. All around the region, it was practically a smorgasbord of spiritual and lifestyle choices, aesthetic practices, and occult excesses, with some Christianity sprinkled in. It was a perpetual first-century self-help convention and trade show. If postmodernism did not start there, it could have.

There is not that much difference today, when you can walk into many Christian bookstores and find every kind of self-help, personal growth, and human-centered gospel to last you five of your best lives now! There are multiple "how-to" books, "secrets-to" books, and "keys-to" everything books. There are "five steps" to this, and "ten steps" to that. There is every conceivable help for "uncovering" this mystery or "unlocking" that door.

For those who want to be rich, happy, wise, wealthy, likeable, blessed with money, deliriously happy, very rich, find their dream (see rich and happy section), go to Mardi Gras with an angel, reach one's potential, visit the third heaven, or be happy because they deserve to be rich, likable, and happy, well,… you get the picture. It makes you wonder how folks survived in days gone by with just a Bible.

On the other hand, for those who want books on repentance, imputation, sanctification, or justification, they usually are not in stock, but they can order it and they will call in two weeks when it is in.

So in an effort to bring the point home, and with a bit of a back-to-the-future theme, let's consider this event from a long time ago and see whether any of it sounds vaguely familiar today.

It is AD 65 and you are the pastor of a small but rapidly growing home church in Colossae. You get a call on a Saturday afternoon from one of your elders who reports that half your church just took a camel carpool over to Laodicea to try the New Age Asian fusion restaurant and wine bar, and then they were planning to take in a lecture from Simon the Kool—a current and very hot semi-divine celeb life coach and cousin to future icon Tony Robbins, 1,900 years removed. They buy all of Kool's latest parchments, including "Discernment is Overrated" and "Channeling Your Best Version of Yourself," both chart-busters on the Gnostic Hot 100. And as if it weren't already a great night, they even manage to get Kool's autograph on their way out of the open-air lobby.

But the evening is still young. So they proceed five miles down the road to Hierapolis because one of the believers in the group had a coupon for a group bath and spa redeemable "for you and six of your friends." That would no doubt be just the perfect way to top off a great evening in the suburbs. As they enter the bath area, one in the group stops at the Coexist Total Health kiosk in the lobby of the spa and picks up an olive oil and pomegranate youth and wisdom enhancer and a copy of the new parchment, "Your Best Life in Antiquity," which the year before had been a runaway bestseller from Athens to Ephesus. They all pass it around while kicking back in the spa and continue the debriefing of Kool's seminar. As they soak in the luxurious mineral hot bath, someone in the group is overheard saying, "It just doesn't get any better than this!" They end their bath and their evening in prayer and warm up the camels for the twenty-mile trek back to Colossae.

As they travel home on a cool, moonlit night, their hearts are full. They alternate between singing songs of praise and social justice anthems from indie and emo artists emerging out of Ephesus.

What a night!

The presence, acceptance, and following of false teachers was so effective in making inroads into the lives and practice of the Christian believers that the apostle Paul, through the Holy Spirit in chapters 1 and 2 of Colossians, powerfully reasserts and reaffirms both the *complete* divinity and the *exclusive* supremacy of Jesus—and Jesus alone!

This amazing proclamation and teaching by Paul was, in part, a defense against false claims of the gospel concerning Jesus that had become pervasive and so injurious to the believers and the church. Church leaders must have had an enormous struggle contending for the truth concerning Jesus and his gospel in that relatively small geographical, three-city region. The pressures had to have been very, very strong. The temptation for many young believers to continue following some of the tantalizing features of the plethora of false teachers presented strong doctrinal challenges.

If Paul's brilliant and complete defense of who Jesus is, in its magnificent presentation as seen in the first two chapters of Colossians, is any measure of the ferocity of the challenge that was present, then that challenge was surely unrelenting and fierce.

Considering the full force of hell behind the designs of evil men who were leading people astray concerning who Jesus was and is, both in Colossae at that time and in our culture today, the words in the first chapter, although familiar, are now seen in a more powerful light:

> He is the image of the invisible God, the firstborn over all creation. For by him all things were created: things in heaven and on earth, visible and invisible, whether thrones or powers or rulers or authorities; all things were created by him and for him. He is before all things, and in him all things hold together. And he is the head of the body, the church; he is the beginning and the firstborn from among the dead, so that in everything he might have the supremacy.
> —Col. 1:15–18 NIV

All around the young church proponents of Greek philosophy and Gnosticism abounded, promising knowledge, fulfillment, serenity from self-discipline, and the first-century version of self-actualization. And all of this occurred while defining Jesus as no different from other semi-divines who had come before him, or those who were in their midst then. Many believers were being drawn in and drawn away from the pure faith.

This is why Paul is so adamant in Colossians 2:8–10 when he magnifies that Jesus is Lord: "See to it that no one takes you captive through hollow and deceptive philosophy, which depends on human tradition and the basic principles of this world rather than on Christ. For in Christ all the fullness of the Deity lives in bodily form, and you have been given fullness in Christ, who is the head over every power and authority" (NIV).

What an amazing articulation of the truth of Christ Jesus to dispel and destroy the lies that had been perpetuated regarding him. I can only picture the scene as Epaphras and the church leaders read that letter aloud the first time to their congregation or maybe on the public square in Colossae.

Paul termed what the heretics were doing to the believers as "plunder," which means something similar to looting or pillaging. It evokes a scene where lawlessness has broken out in an area, where shops and stores have their merchandise strewn all over the ground while thieves pick through and take the things that are most valuable. This is a description of the fruit of heresy. This is what toleration of "another gospel" looks like. The proclaimed Word of God is truly the anointing that breaks every yoke and clears the street of looters.

Passing the Torch of Truth

Toward the end of Paul's ministry and life, the zeal he possessed and wanted urgently to transfer to his protégé, Timothy, centered to a great degree on upholding and defending the soundness of the teachings concerning the gospel. A brief look once again at Paul's letters to Timothy is timely.

The heart of both letters reveals a keen urgency on the part of Paul, as the apostle's exhortations to Timothy appeal to the young preacher to "hold fast" to the truth of the messages and teachings. In 2 Timothy alone there are over a dozen uses of the word *doctrine* or *teaching* as the apostle implores Timothy to safeguard the gospel and its very clear mandates.

The story is the same. The false teachers were so prevalent and doing so much damage to the young church that the apostle steps up his defense by naming names and identifying specific offenses, while calling for prohibitions against individuals who were engaged in "overthrowing the faith of some."

Rhetorically speaking, how did they do it? How were the false teachers so successful in leading so many people astray at a time when the gospel message was setting the known world ablaze? Even more pertinent, how has the church today made itself so vulnerable and susceptible to the perils of false teaching?

These questions matter because false teachers produce false converts. Moreover, that equation is interchangeable: False converts also produce false teachers. Is it the chicken or the egg that comes first, or does it really matter? The Bible gives us clear insight on how both are created and rise from among the church. These passages speak directly to what constitutes the making of false teachers and false converts:

> Nor give heed to fables and endless genealogies, which cause disputes rather than godly edification which is in faith. Now the purpose of the commandment is love form a pure heart, from a good conscience, and form sincere faith, from which some, having strayed, have turned aside to idle talk, desiring to be teachers of the law understanding neither what they say nor the things which they affirm.
>
> —1 Tim. 1:4–7

> Now the Spirit says that in latter times some will depart from the faith, giving heed to deceiving sprits and doctrines of demons, speaking lies in hypocrisy, having their own conscience seared with a hot iron, forbidding to marry, and commanding to abstain from foods which God created to be received with thanksgiving by those who believe and know the truth.
>
> —1 Tim. 4:1–3

> If anyone teaches otherwise and does not consent to wholesome words, *even* the words of our Lord Jesus Christ, and to the doctrine which accords with godliness, he is

proud, knowing nothing, but is obsessed with disputes and arguments over words, from which come envy, strife, reviling, evil suspicions, useless wrangling of men of corrupt minds and destitute of the truth, who suppose that godliness is a means of gain. From such withdraw yourself.

—1 Tim. 6:3–5

For men will be lovers of themselves, lovers of money, boasters, proud, blasphemers, disobedient to parents, unthankful, unholy, unloving, unforgiving, slanderers of good, traitors, headstrong, haughty, lovers of pleasure rather than lovers of God, having a form of godliness but denying its power. And from such people turn away!

—2 Tim. 3:2–5

Now I urge you, brethren, note those who cause division and offenses, contrary to the doctrine which you learned, and avoid them. For those who are such do not serve our Lord Jesus Christ, but their own belly, and by smooth words and flattering speech deceive the hearts of the simple.

—Rom. 16:17–18

For the time will come when they will not endure sound doctrine, but according to their own desires, because they have itching ears, they will heap up for themselves teachers, and they will turn their ears away from the truth, and be turned aside to fables.

—2 Tim. 4: 3–4

Those by the wayside are the ones who hear; then the devil comes and takes away the word out of their hearts, lest they should believe and be saved. But the ones on the rock are those who, when they hear, receive the word with great joy; and these have no root, who believe for awhile and in time of temptation fall away. Now the ones that fell among thorns are those who, when they have heard, go out and are choked with cares, riches, and pleasures of life, and bring no fruit to maturity.

—Luke 8:12–14

These kinds of scenes repeated themselves wherever the gospel was taken. However, through the power of the Holy Spirit and the resolve of the godly to reiterate and elevate the important doctrines of the young church, we see in part how the church overcame (and overcomes today) the obstacles of "another gospel." It is the proclamation, teaching, and emphasis of the Word that continues to be our forward weapon in the battle for truth.

Welcome, Christian, to the postmodern battlefield. God has you here now—at this moment—in this age. You are not a passive player by design, for you have been called for such a time as this.

There is a scene in *The Two Towers,* the second of Peter Jackson's blockbuster films in The Lord of the Rings series, that I would borrow (without necessarily assigning spiritual significance) to enhance the point. King Théoden and Aragorn are discussing the prospects of battle as news is received of the Orcs bearing down on the king's people in Rohan. Théoden, seeking to expose neither his army nor his people to disaster, declares to Aragorn, "I will not risk open warfare." Aragorn intently replies, "War is upon you, whether you risk it or not!"

Besides being a great line, Aragorn's comment is descriptive of the contemporary times. The battle is joined and we see the truth that war is at hand. And make no mistake, this is a war whether we want it or not—a war for explicit biblical truth. Nevertheless, the very power we possess as Christians is derived from the truth of God's Word. And this remains a war for truth. It is not about personalities; it is about principalities.

It must be waged with an unrelenting faith and passionate resolve to see that the teachings of the gospel of Jesus Christ are proclaimed as timeless, transcendent truths, immovable and unchangeable by the whims and deceptions of the Devil, his demons, and heretical false teachers.

One of the ways we know we are in a war is that we will encounter increased persecution. In America, what we call persecution so far has been mild compared to the persecution of Christians in many other parts of the world. Maybe we face criticism and perhaps a little embarrassment—a cultural fear that we will be labeled intolerant or judgmental. But that is going to change. It is going to increase to greater intensity because that is the way the culture and God's timeline is heading.

Ultimately, we are not at war with individuals and we do not aim to target people as the enemy. We are reminded in Ephesians 6:12 who the real enemy is: "For our struggle is not against flesh and blood, but against the rulers, against the authorities, against the powers of this dark world and against the spiritual forces of evil in the heavenly realms" (NIV). Our weapon in this struggle is the proclamation of God's Word—the objective truth for which it is—and we must proclaim it. It is our calling as Christian believers. This is not a movie, and there is much more at stake than an Oscar. This is life and war for truth in the postmodern church. The Word of God is the sword of the Spirit.

Strap it on!

The Utter Irrelevance of Cultural Relevance

I still think Jesus is cool. In a trendy sort of way.
—Pamela Anderson, actress, 2004

IF THERE IS anything that has become the Holy Grail of quests in the postmodern church, it is finding the secret to cultural relevance. It seems to be an equal opportunity venture, with just about every stream of Christianity hot on the trail in pursuit of ... *it*!

What is *it*?

I have been with other pastors and friends and I have heard it lauded, argued, defended, offended, criticized, marginalized, demonized, and sanitized. I have also read numerous books and articles on *it*. But I am still unable to find any consensus on what *it* actually is.

I wish to distinguish *it* from agreement that ministering to different people groups or demographic groups requires knowledge of cultural distinctions in order to be effective. To the extent that cultural relevance is defined in that context, I have no quarrel. Such things as distinguishing language and customs within other nationalities and ethnic groups would be imperative to know in light of the extreme differences that exist. But I am referring to cultural relevance as the elusive gem of the American church pursuit targeting unchurched people to come to grow our church. My question is, "To what end?" I ask that question often because the answer, or lack of any clear answer, is the crux of why relevance is sought.

Making the Culture more Comfortable

There are three reasons I recoil at the generic and unqualified use of the term "cultural relevancy" as a pursuit in the church. The first is when a church desires so much to be relevant that it resorts to an intentional effort that looks like an extreme church makeover. Everything is seemingly transformed in program and emphasis—and even language—to reflect awareness that we have a handle on making the unsaved culture comfortable with their surroundings. We do practically everything to disarm the culture with our presentation of the "gospel" to communicate how relevant we are. On the surface, that seems like a reasonable course of action. But why? What is our ultimate motive? Even if the pastor dresses down and the worship leader turns it up, do we really believe that somehow they will experience a softer landing when we proclaim both the gospel promises and gospel warnings of Jesus? Does the true message become more palatable when we try making the culture more comfortable with their surroundings in church? Does it matter whether someone comes to the traditional service or the contemporary service if we preach a compromising gospel? Do we want to see our "hip" quotient rise when the pastor announces the beginning of a six-week series on discerning the voice of God through an expository look at season four of *The Simpsons*? The church attendance will likely increase, but then typically what happens is that the church reaches a fork in the road, where either the forward momentum of the relevancy-growth train will leave the station and require more and more relevancy fuel to keep the growth chugging along. Or, the gospel will be preached and the orthodox teachings of the church will be taught, and those who will be saved will stay, and those who are lost or have grown cold will leave and not come back. And this will happen whether the music is great or not. So why are we doing all this?

I am not talking about the perils of dressing casually and I am not being critical for making people feel comfortable. Since 1992 I have worn blue jeans and sandals to work almost exclusively. It is comfortable. But more importantly, it has been appropriate for the ministry culture of which I have been a part. And if I work in a ministry or secular career that calls for a shirt and tie, I will order the light starch at the cleaners and comply. A shirt and tie will undoubtedly look good with sandals.

I have retained all my "power ties" from the 1980s, from before I went into ministry, saving them in the event this happens. Until then, they are generally reserved for weddings, funerals, and movie premiers, which total about twenty-five since 1992. Twenty-five, that is, if you count the movie premiers. (For the benefit of those who don't get *The Matrix*, I am pointing to the fact that I have never been to a movie premier.)

What I am suggesting here is that cultural relevance, as a conscious change to attract the culture that is part of a plan to show relevancy for relevancy's sake, may need to be reevaluated. Churches emphasizing external aesthetics, cultural props, and contemporary presentation in hopes of creating a relevant vibe for people they are trying to attract should ask the question over and over: For what ultimate purpose? To grow in relevance as demonstrated by increases in attendance of the target audience? Or to preach Christ's gospel and let the attendance chips fall where they may? Does it really matter in the end (I mean in the judgment sense of the phrase) that someone attended a great family church for twenty years but never heard the concepts of repentance, atonement for sin, or judgment even mentioned, never mind taught? If it takes the "dancing bears" to draw people, it will require the "dancing bears" to keep people.

The God Squad to the Rescue

The second reason I advocate using caution and encourage the need for clarity when talking about cultural relevancy has to do with my own self-serving venture into relevancy while in college. It was my first conscious foray into the concept of being relevant.

It was during the first week of fall quarter of my junior year, and I was sitting in a philosophy class with thirteen or fourteen other upperclassmen. The professor broke us into small discussion groups for the term and I volunteered to be part of what he called the "God Squad" group, which would be my small discussion group for in-class debates, whereby our team would advocate for the position of God in all philosophical arguments.

The professor then made an in-class assignment, due in fifteen minutes, asking the class to write down and be ready to recite in no more than two words an answer to the question, "How would you describe your concept of God?"

This was my moment. And it was happening the very first day! Here was my opportunity to say something profound, something that would show I was in touch with God and would demonstrate how cool and relevant both he and I were. It was not the season in my life when humility and dying to self were having their finest hour.

I knew that to really wow everybody I had to answer in one word, not the two words allowed, much like the old game show *Name That Tune* in which the fewer notes it took to name the tune the more Mr. Microphones and Chia pets you won. Anyway, I knew if I could come up with one profound adjective, the class would be impressed with both me and God—sadly, in that order of priority. My brilliant response could redefine what it meant to be both chic *and* religious, which would surely take me over the top as I would certainly lauded by my intellectual classmates for the rest of the quarter.

So when it was my turn, the professor looked at me and said, "Mr. Babb, what is your response?"

I paused a bit for dramatic effect, and said, "Positivism."

And then I got the two or three affirming oohs and ahhhs that signaled my success and acceptance. Mission accomplished. I was the king of cool.

Then almost immediately, I began to go from elation to disappointment. As the class ended and I left with the day dragging on, I started to feel empty and slightly depressed. As I thought about what I had said, I wondered how God felt about how I had described him. Looking back at that time, it was probably a sure bet that I was not a believer, although I would have told you I was, even with most evidence of my life to the contrary. At the time I thought I could be some kind of cool religious influence on the God-hating students. I really thought that. Because after all, if they liked me, then they may be open to liking Jesus. I was sure I could make him relevant to them today. I was sure of this because the Jesus I would have given them would not have cost them a thing. And the reality is, I really did not get around to talking about the biblical Jesus that much because I had a very fundamental problem: It was impossible to effectively share what I was *not living*. I may have been unofficially relevant for that term in school, but I was officially irrelevant in my day-to-day "almost Christian" walk. The other small groups attacked our impotent little God Squad for the rest of the semester, always putting us on the defensive. You can only argue a metaphysical god so much. None of us were dedicated believers who followed Christ as real disciples. The Bible was off limits to reference as well. Talk about going to a gunfight without bullets. We single-handedly, in that one semester, set Christian apologetics back to the Ice Age.

Now, one could conclude that this episode was more a product of my need to be popular and acceptable to people than a desire to be relevant. But in the context of a generation that views generic relevance as acceptance, it is really a distinction without a difference. In the final analysis, they are basically the same.

I submit that for far too many churches in the postmodern era, relevancy and acceptance appear to be fairly interchangeable. All too often, acceptance does not mean we will be heard, but only that we will be tolerated. And how do we know which motive is at work? How does the postmodern church make the distinction between relevance for the sake of the gospel and relevance for the sake of institutional acceptance?

The answer comes in how and what is being proclaimed as the true gospel of Christ. And that includes not just a biblical proclamation of salvation, but teaching the believer the meaning and importance of their conversion, as well as the doctrines of the faith. It is the grounding in these doctrines that our congregations are growing further and further away from in both knowledge and application. Instead, there are too many who are looking for "ooh" and "ahh" affirmations, as I did in college—and far too often have done in ministry.

The Claims Jesus Makes about Himself

The third and most important reason for my reluctance about Christianity embracing cultural relevancy is the crux of the very message of the gospel. Jesus bears little or no resemblance to the culture. He transcends the culture, even the postmodern culture, and because he is nothing like the culture, he is therefore extremely relevant to the culture to which he bears no resemblance.

How is that?

Because of who Jesus is. His relevance is confirmed in the fact that regardless of cultural context, he is Messiah, Savior, and Lord—the only way to God. That is all a bit too exclusivist for the culture, but it is nevertheless the relevant point because it is true.

It would probably be good to ask some questions about how we apply our view of cultural relevance in the church. Is it defined as making Jesus himself culturally relevant? Is it the *message* of Jesus that we must make relevant? And if so, how do we make it relevant while at the same time proclaiming its power to redeem, when its very claims are so antithetical to the culture? Can it be dosed out? Or is it the church itself that we must make relevant through some redefined contemporary mission?

You can read dozens of articles on what defines cultural relevancy in the church, and you can find dozens of variations on their meaning. It would be easier to do a television miniseries on the life and times of Enoch: "And Enoch walked with God; and he was not, for God took him" (Gen. 5:24). But a more important question still remains: "Could relevancy really be a sort of pretense for our desire for acceptance *by* the culture—and if so, to what end?"

Jesus states plainly that "If the world hates you, keep in mind that it hated me first" (John 15:18 NIV).

Why?

Because of the claims Jesus makes about himself, which are confirmed through the prophets who came long before him, the eyewitnesses who walked with him, and two thousand years of believers who have come after him. If we are proclaiming the historical Jesus, then it is the claims themselves that are relevant—irrespective of our need to find a cultural context. Jesus and his claims *are* the cultural context, and the Lord promises us that in so proclaiming we are likely to be passed over when the culture gives out "good guy" awards.

As Christians we have to answer the question of whether *relevancy* is actually a synonym for the *acceptance* that we covet. Are we trying to be acceptable or liked by the culture instead of proclaiming the gospel truth to the culture? Doing that will elicit disdain from the culture on a broad scale, as certain as disco ruined radio in the 1970s. Yet at the same time, we can be assured that "whosoever" in that same culture will be rescued by that gospel proclamation.

Who or what are we trying to make relevant? Is it us, our churches, our message, or Jesus? And if it is our message, what strategies do we employ to make the message more acceptable to an unbelieving culture? Because if, in the attempt to be heard, we render the message impotent by excluding its truth claims, we may win some accolades, but we may lose the soul of the very culture we desire to salvage.

Perhaps at the core of the whole relevancy issue is a more fundamental truth that cannot be cleaned up or sanitized regardless of methodology. The true gospel is a completely and utterly scandalous message, with Jesus as the centrality of both that message and its offense—a message that cannot be consistent with a desire to please the culture. The truth may set them free, but it will hack them off first. Enough so that most will walk away in great offense.

The True Gospel Is Offensive

Martin Luther said, "God forbid that the offense of the Cross ever be removed." He said that because if the offense is removed, its power is taken away.

Paul calls the message of the gospel a "scandal," something that the Jews stumble over and the Gentile world (Greeks) deems as "foolishness." The apostle also makes several references in his letters about his not being ashamed of the gospel, indicating that great difficulty accompanies its preaching and living it out. He just affirms that shame is not a barrier for his proclamation.

Where do the shame, the offense, and the scandal originate?

They come from the assessment of those in the whole universe of the culture, the entire world system of unbelief that populates the planet and that has codified the notion of the insanity of the message of the cross from age to age. This postmodern age has made its declaration, as well. The question before us is whether a church in the postmodern age is seeking to remove the offense in order to be seen as more tolerant and less rigid, thereby becoming more "relevant."

A closer look at the significance of Paul's claim of not being ashamed of the gospel contains a staggering revelation. On its face, the statement seems to be a great example for the believer to emulate. To walk in a manner that we are not ashamed of Christ and his cross is a noble and worthy desire, something we would aspire to in our lives as believers. Yet with Paul, the proclamation becomes incredibly powerful and relevant, because if anyone had a reason to be ashamed, it was Paul, as he had given his entire life to being a studied and legalistic Jew. He was without peer in knowledge of the law, and as a Pharisee he was in the elite class. He would be the Albert Einstein of the law.

Imagine the tight culture of his friends, his peers, and his lifetime associates. Then Paul encounters Jesus and is saved and called to preach the gospel in many instances to that same fraternity. Imagine coming back to his former associates, who were zealous in their protection of keeping the very heresies away that one of their favored sons was now preaching. The gospel was a direct contradiction of everything Paul believed concerning the Messiah. And now he is proclaiming it with fervency in order to see his former brothers saved by that very gospel. They must have thought he had gone mad.

What Paul was preaching was so scandalous, so offensive, that it became something the Jews tripped over and could not get past. They all knew the circumstances involving the birth of

Jesus, which was itself a scandal. They argued that the Messiah could not come out of Nazareth. They knew his family was not one of any distinction. The list of preconceived objections against Jesus as the Chosen One went on and on. It did not fit the paradigm, to say the least. It was utter madness to Paul's lifelong associates. Worse than that, it was blasphemy!

Yet Paul was eager and concerned for his former associates to come to Christ, as can be read in the ninth and tenth chapters of Romans.

But there's more. After traveling closer to home, it is on to Athens, the great cultural center of knowledge, reason, and philosophy. It is there that the sages of the time ridiculed Paul and called him a "babbler," which is recorded in chapter 17 of the book of Acts.

Paul proclaimed the uncompromising gospel in another amazing presentation to the intelligentsia in Athens, and a few people who heard the message wanted to hear more. Some were even saved. But the account is clear that Paul was mocked and ridiculed for what seemed to be a ridiculous claim that repentance is demanded by a "foreign god"—said to be the heavenly Father of some man from the outback of nowhere, who was sentenced to a criminal's death in a garbage dump—and that trusting in him would secure the passage for the salvation of their souls. It is a notion that was absurd, because it is absurd! After all, these were intelligent, reasonable sages, the best the world had to offer. What a fool, this Paul!

And if we as professing believers do not embrace the scandal of that same gospel today, then we become susceptible to "another gospel." But hold on, the shame grows larger still.

Paul was also a Roman citizen. And even though it was the bidding of the religious power brokers who brought Jesus to a kangaroo court, it was a hideous implement of Roman capital punishment that facilitated the death sentence of Jesus. It is also accounted in Roman antiquity that the cross as a means of execution was such a humiliating, shameful, disgusting, and scandalous occurrence, it was deemed inappropriate and out of bounds for decent people to even mention in conversation. It was considered rude and barbaric to speak freely of its atrociousness in public, as would be the case about any scandal.

Paul, the Roman citizen, the Jew of Jews, preached the scandal until he was executed in the very city of his natural citizenship. He openly delighted in the merits of the scandalous cross, thereby distorting and disturbing the cultural mores of any decent citizen of Rome.

So when the apostle says to the church at Galatia and to Timothy, "I am not ashamed of the gospel," he says it with a conviction that is born out of the power of that gospel's full measure of offense, shame, and scandal. That is why he goes on to proclaim, "It is the power of God unto salvation."

Today, in postmodern civilization, the gospel is even more scandalous and offensive. It is a scandal because it calls people to the fact that they have no ability—none—to save themselves by the futility of their good works. It is offensive because it proclaims to a culture the exclusivity of Jesus as the *only way by which anyone is saved,* and that faith in Christ cannot be compromised to an "all roads lead to the same destination" cultural conclusion.

It is disgusting to the culture because it asserts that a bloody and violent cross is the means by which the Savior willingly took onto himself the holy wrath of God to assuage the sin of humankind. And we must embrace the merits of that hideous and shameful cross. It is only through the blood shed on the cross that men and women are justified before God. It is revolting because the crucifixion of Christ on the cross is the very act that precipitates the belief in the physical and spiritual resurrection of Jesus, the firstfruits of victory over death. For the majority of people in the culture, this is a fairy tale. But for believers, it is the foundational truth claim of all history.

The gospel is absurd to an age that prides itself in the celebration of human effort, secular and religious ecumenical enlightment, because it forces the age to bow in acknowledgment of the one true God of the universe—something that, by definition, prideful men and women will not bring themselves to do. If we want to be culturally relevant with a gospel that is relevant, then we are compelled to preach its offense and scandal, because it is in that very proclamation that humans are confronted with what they must do with that offense. People either will not get past the gospel's absurdity, or in humility they will embrace its saving merits.

Therein lies the power of the gospel to rescue humanity, and so it must be proclaimed. Anything else in its place is our version of babbling.

A gospel without the scandal is just "another gospel."

Can't We All Just Get Along?

The thing about cultural relevance, however you choose to define what it means, is that there is no *it* without the scandal and offense of the message. And that is true no matter how you change the setting. This fact is not going to put a sunshine face on Mr. Culture, who will constantly remind us that we do not work and play well with others. This presents an immediate dilemma for which we are confronted as believers in ministry, because we all know that the culture defines relevance as something that is *not* offensive, exclusive, or dogmatic, and most of all, not judgmental. Uh-oh.

This brings us to another problem. What do we say when we are telling the gospel? How do we say it? We do not want to be jerks about it, for it is true that the gospel is offensive enough without delivering its message it like Rosanne Barr singing the National Anthem. But in the end that will be a red herring anyway, a diversion to shame us into not preaching the scandal, because that is always the true reason for strenuous cultural objections.

So no matter what our preoccupation is with how to get the culture to listen, we are still going to have to give them some very, very bad news. Then, and only then—*especially* then—is the good news very good. In the end, it is the offensive message of the true gospel that is singularly relevant, because it is the only thing in the culture that can save the culture.

And that makes *it*, the gospel, extremely relevant.

Signs of the Times

We recently moved back to the south after nine years in California. Before that time, I had lived somewhere in Tennessee all my forty-four years until the Lord moved us out west for nine really great years of ministry in the Bay area.

There are five things you notice about the south after having been away for any length of time. These five things are instantly and indelibly etched in your mind. First, the humidity; second, the people in that region are the friendliest, by far; third, there is no such thing as a bad "Meat and Three;" fourth, the west coast has no Krystal's or Waffle House; and fifth, because of my rediscovery of numbers two, three, and four, I have now become an expert on statin medications, triglycerides, and acceptable LDL (bad cholesterol).

There is another phenomenon seen in the south that is quite a bit rarer on the west coast, and that is the church message sign. I had not forgotten that there is almost literally a church on every corner in the southern region of America, but coming back and actually seeing them all over the place still took some getting used to. This is not to imply, by the way, that because there are more churches in the south that it necessarily translates to more Christians. It just means there are probably more in the south who think they are Christians, which may not be such a hot distinction. My eighteen-year-old son, who was born in the south but raised for over half his life in California, was particularly blown away by the churches and their marquee signs. The first couple of weeks back, he and I would drive around the area and read the signs, which demonstrated not only how little it took for us to be entertained but also the urgent need for us to get a life.

There is some very interesting theology on church signs, as well as much insight into what is valued at a church. Pursuant to that, some of the messages leave me wondering why God does not allow some of the signs to get lifted, but then I recall the wheat and the tares.

There is something fundamental that has happened over the last decade to church signage in general. I suspect it is following on the heels of the desire for relevancy. Unless you already have prior knowledge, I find that you have to guess what kind of church you are looking at because of how they have come up with their name. It is like trying to solve a mystery. With the exception of a few denominational churches with pre-Civil War buildings, most of the time I have to go inside and ask the secretary, "What kind of church is this?"

"Oh, we're a Christian church."

"No, ma'am. I mean, are you denominational, formally denominational, independent, charismatic … what?"

"We are a Bible-believing church."

"Yes, ma'am. I'm just trying to find out if you have an affiliation with an evangelical association or denomination. Were you part of something before? Or has the church always been called the Glorious and Thunderous Rose?"

"The pastor's not here or you could talk to him, but would you like to have a brochure with our Web site on it?"

"I appreciate your help, ma'am. Can I speak with the custodian?"

What is it with these names? Why don't we just identify what kind of church we are? Are we trying so hard not to *be church* that we now think we can *do church* and fool people into coming because somehow our cute name leaves them guessing about what we are? Is that being culturally relevant? Is the strip mall shopping center with the sign saying "The Place: Happy Hour, 11 AM" talking about beer on tap, Texas hold 'em, or is it a church?

I get the theory: "We drop the church language because many of the people we are trying to reach have had bad church experiences." I just wonder how much you are going to have to drop or compromise the gospel message to keep the hurt people. This is the relevant point: We are so muting the message of the cross in order to be seen as culturally acceptable that we are creating an entire church culture of congregants who are not only reluctant to share their faith, but have little idea *how* to do it. Add on the pressure from the culture to minimize professions of "knowing" anything for certain, and it just becomes easier to shut up and keep your religion to yourself. That must have come around the same time as the gospel of "don't talk politics or religion," which we're all reminded of frequently.

Jesus Christ is relevant because of who he is and his inseparable message. If we try to disconnect one from another, Jesus may become cool and trendy because of how we have tried to sell him to the culture, but his Word will still be all the more relevant.

> He has appeared to put away sin by the sacrifice of Himself. And as it is appointed for men to die once, but after this the judgment, so Christ was offered once to bear the sins of many. To those who eagerly wait for Him, He will appear a second time, apart from sin, for salvation.
> —Heb. 9:26b–28 NKJV

Cultural relevance has gone full throttle as our churches scramble to come up with methods to help shape our message in a postmodern world. It would be nice to ease off the throttle just a bit and make sure the methods are not trumping the message, the true message. Cultural relevance has almost become a brand in postmodern Christianity, almost the third rail of doctrine in many cases.

And the brand has never been more validated than in what has become an entire church movement where we assume people are "seeking" for a divine purpose and pursuit of God.

Seeker Ye First the Kingdom of Felt Needs

My felt needs—trump old creeds
Orthodoxy dry as a bone!
Sensitive seekers—with "easy bake" preachers—
"How do we keep our grass green?"
Gospel message left the scene!

—Postmodern Hymn #915

IN THE WINTER of 2001, Frank moved to Southern California from Pennsylvania with his wife and three children. They had been looking for a church home but were not able to find a place to sink roots. Frank grew up as a Lutheran, but he found himself drifting away from the denomination as he got older. When he and Connie married they became involved with larger conservative evangelical churches. But having heard so much about "seeker sensitive churches," he thought to himself, *Why not go and try it? We're in a new place and we ought to do it.*

Frank procrastinated for a while because he and Connie were really trying to keep the priority on finding a home church.

But about three months later, still not having found a place, they decided to give the seeker big-box church a go. Frank and Connie were curious because they had read so much about seeker stuff and they wanted to get a flavor for it. They wanted to find out, once and for all, if Bill Hybels of Willow Creek fame, and Rick Warren, Mr. Purpose Driven Everything—two icons of the seeker and market-driven model—really did grow fangs at midnight and howl at the moon!

Or had they tapped into a great way to reach people for Jesus?

The church in question was one of three seeker giants within about thirty-five miles of each other, so they picked the one nearest to their home and set off on their excellent church adventure one cool Sunday morning in February.

Let's hear the story as if in Frank's words.

I parked the car and we went inside the lobby. It looked like the Supernova *Starbucks* had crashed and exploded in the place! Boy, did it smell great!

I'm talking hundreds of people standing around at countless coffee dispensers, sitting at tables and on tables, with music blasting. I have nothing against serving coffee; I've just never walked into a church before, having my very first thought be "good to the last drop."

Great fellowship was happening everywhere, and everyone was so incredibly nice. We were only one family among many visiting couples and families, yet we were all attended to with a great sense of caring, getting directions for our children, and so on. While multitudes of people slammed down rivers of java, one concern kept running the circuit in my mind: "I hope this place has monitors in the restrooms so people will actually get to experience the service."

The conversation was fast, furious, and loud, which led me to conclude that they had run out of decaf that morning in fairly short order.

My family and I were greeted very warmly at one of the many information kiosks, and I was given a packet that includes a couple of dozen small group notices that are open. While my wife strolled around hunting for a low-fat double-shot espresso without foam, I took a glance at the lineup that featured the small group topics.

I was struck with the advanced nature of the topics. They included some topics I wasn't sure even Oprah had broached yet, including, "Relationship Recovery for Adult Children of Trekee Conventioneers."

I had just never seen this growing up a Lutheran. Where I went to church you were lucky to get a Dixie cup of tap water and a stale wafer that hadn't already been used at the Christmas Eve Communion service. And as far as small groups, we never had one unless it was formed as a posse to run the pastor out of town.

But we finally made it into the main hall, along with 1,200 other people, and very quickly there was not a seat left in the house, which I found incredible given the volume of coffee that had been consumed. I figured my goal for the day was to juggle a balance between worshiping God and checking out the vibe of the place.

The band was just coming onstage. They geared up, counted off, and the place erupted into applause as the first notes of U2's "It's a Beautiful Day" were hammered out. Yet before the first chorus was sung, about half of the hall sat down and were just listening and mouthing the words. But when the chorus started they exploded up from their seats once again in thunderous applause and shouts. A few people could be heard singing the chorus, but most were just really enjoying themselves listening to the band, which was absolutely amazing.

They finished the U2 classic and started another song that I had not heard, but many people seemed to know it, and there was much more participation, maybe about seventy-five percent. I can't recall anything about the song other than it was a blues thing about joy. I just didn't recognize it.

Then they began the third song, which was the classic "Fame" by David Bowie. Again the band nailed it and the crowd loved it! Trouble was, have you ever tried singing, let alone worshiping, to the song "Fame?" I mean, you're presented with some real decisions you have to make very quickly. Do you take the background vocals that are doing the Pet Shop Boys/Depeche Mode thing, or do you try and sing the melody and follow Dave's unique Euro-dance lead vocal part? I'm thinking, *Okay we're going to cover this song with Christian lyrics, right? It's hard to sing, but I'm down with this—I can go for it*!

Then the band started singing the actual words to the actual song. The band was—the congregation would have injured themselves trying to sing.

By now, I was convinced we had the wrong address and we were actually at some corporate coffee drink-off with some incredible live music providing the background, and at any moment this great grand prize was going to be given away for the one who holds out going to the bathroom the longest. I figured that, at that point, we would stay because maybe they'd be giving out a door prize or something.

It was also around the time the band was in the instrumental outro that I began to ponder Warren's mega-seller *Purpose-Driven Church*, trying to recall in which chapter this experience was chronicled. Then it was over—the worship, that is.

Fifteen minutes had passed and the band was off the stage faster than the Stones trying to get out of the Altamont in '69! I'm thinking, *Maybe that was the sound check?* But that would be wrong.

As fast as the band left, a small army of a crew set up the stage in what seemed to be no more than a minute. Then a drama team of teens and adults came on and did this sort of half-mime, half-dialogue skit/drama that I was hoping was some kind of introduction to the door prize giveaway, but my wife said it had something to do with telling a story about the price of "Fame."

"Now that's cool," I said to myself. "I see a kind of thematic weaving thing happening."

In three minutes they were gone and someone else came out to give a brief announcement about the short video we were about to see, which were the real announcements. It was very well done and very informative about what was going on in the life of the church. It was here that the emcee also mentioned something about a midweek service that was designed for people to go deeper into studies of the Bible. Speaking of which, I also took notice of how many people brought their Bibles. What do you think?

The announcements concluded with the giant video screen rising up and the house lights dimming a bit. The pastor walked onstage and delivered an eighteen-minute talk on, you guessed it, fame. I don't recall if there were references to Scripture or Jesus because I spent most of those eighteen minutes trying to find a suitable vocal part in my mind for the band's cover during worship.

The pastor concluded the talk and began the process of taking an offering—barely. I say barely because the pastor, according to Connie, after being incredibly engaging about the perils of fame, turned a bit sour and even threatening when it came to his instructions on giving to the offering. I almost felt as though there was a sanction against giving if I hadn't been drinking coffee there for at least a year. I had never been encouraged so much *not* to give! I felt like I had been told to go to my room, yet I was trying to be understanding that he was making a point about not hounding anyone for money. Got it, pal.

The band played an instrumental during the offering, and at the end we were all dismissed with a prayer, which served as a reminder that I was in an actual church service.

We went out to the lobby, and the great exchange began. There was another 1,200 people coming in for the next service. The precision and timing of herding 2,400 people in and out so efficiently and so impressively in the presence of coffee left me wishing the DMV or post office would come and take notes. We walked out of there with info packets, satisfaction survey cards, a CD by the band featuring 80's classics, and a small book by the pastor. I guess it was consolation for not winning the door prize, but nice nevertheless.

At this point, the sensory overload had me wanting to go to Disneyland on toddler's day just to dial down. Plus "Fame" was going off in my head, and I knew it was going to be a two-month deal before I quit lying in bed trying to get it out of my head.

Yet as we got into the car, some nice parking attendant asked, "How did you enjoy the service?"

"It was good," we said, "but there sure was a lot happening in a small space of time."

He responded very warmly and excitedly by saying, "If you think that was good, you ought to come to our 'seeker' service at 11:00!"

> You see, we will not offend you—
> Cuz we got only good news—
> Stumbling blocks are old school,
> Feeling bad just isn't cool!
>
> —Postmodern Hymn #915

I am not endorsing not pursuing a prayerful emphasis upon methodology in reaching the lost, unless and until that methodology creates an overdeveloped emphasis that begins to compromise the importance of the message. (By the way, what again is the message?) And that, I am afraid, is what is happening at an alarming rate with much of the seeker emphasis.

Jesus Does Not just Complete our Lives

The seeker-sensitive emphasis looks like it is a plan designed for winning the lost by first emphasizing their felt needs and then getting them saved. That may be a great intention and a fine strategy, but a funny thing happened on the way to two-and-a-half kids, a chocolate brown lab, and life-is-good-in-the-burbs. The actual true gospel too much of the time does not actually get around to being proclaimed to the lost. They do not hear the message of who God is, who we are not, repentance, taking up your cross, and the rest.

Worse, a more palatable version of the gospel often gets filtered and doled out in the form of Jesus completing you, or Jesus solving your problems, or the gospel as good news for your relationship problems, career challenges, spouse, and children issues. Like a postcard, none of that is untrue, but it just does not emphasize the real truth of the whole matter. And that is that the gospel is good news because we are compelled by the whole counsel of God to give seekers and others the really, really, really bad news … for real!

How many times do you hear a cultural icon like a sports figure, a rock star, or movie actor talk about Jesus, and when they do they talk about their need to complete their lives, or that something was missing and Jesus filled the void in their lives, or that he became a key for their happiness because "something was not quite right." All of that is partly true, yet it understates the problem by an eternal mile!

The claims of the Bible assert a more critical picture of yours and my status (see chapter 10). Jesus does not just complete our lives—our lives are already complete; by which I mean we are *completely dead*. We are spiritual corpses for which there is no resuscitation. We have no real life without him, none at all. Only when we are told the whole truth does the good news of the gospel actually become good news.

When Jesus told Nicodemus that he "must be born again," he was saying that cleanup projects are not adequate to attain eternal life. Jesus told him he could not bring any reclamation project (flesh) to the table because he had to be completely born again. Nothing could be partially fixed, mended, counseled, or self-actualized. "That which is born of the flesh is flesh, and that which is born of the Spirit is spirit" (John 3:6 NKJV). As Paul Washer has said, "Jesus is not a Yuppie accessory—not a cherry on top; he's not a flu shot!" Jesus and his gospel are everything!

The Vernacular Switch

It is funny how, in an attempt to present the church as less offensive and more tolerant, the seeker movement has changed even the vernacular of the contemporary church. An example of this kind of language change is that the formerly "unsaved" are now the "unchurched." After all, we do not want to label or alienate them, or have them feeling weird in general about the prospect of dying in their sins and going to hell for all eternity.

With this kind of semantics switch important questions arise. For example, does this mean that the unsaved who populate congregations in all kinds of churches are now the new "churched," and that the "old saved," who were formerly not acknowledged during this change in culture and language, are now the "old churched" who are saved but have no other name to go by, because the "new unsaved churched" already have the "new churched" label? And if so, which Sunday school class do I go to?

Is there no way to have an intermediate status in this system? The Catholics have purgatory. Why can't the seekers have a class if they are agnostic or unsure about whether they are saved and unchurched, or unsaved and churched, twice removed? Is there a class for the once saved, always formerly churched? And where does the person go who is now formerly unsaved, but was told by the pastor that he is not unsaved but rather just unchurched? Should he throw up his hands and heed the pastor's advice, "Don't worry, be happy?"

No wonder everybody is in the lobby drinking coffee. They don't have a clue where to go to Sunday school! Except that is no longer a problem because in most cases there is no longer Sunday school by name or reality. Actual Sunday school is nearly extinct in the seeker movement.

And why is that? Because we base the method of our message upon cultural assumptions about those to whom we minister. We have concluded that busy suburban families will not invest the time in Sunday school, so we acknowledge that felt need and design accordingly. Besides, we've expended all this resource and manpower for this amazing fifty-minute corporate gig.

Could it be that if the gospel were actually proclaimed, as Paul said, "in demonstration of the Spirit and in power," and that that was our actual emphasis, some of the cultural assumptions could perhaps be transcended by that message? Does the true gospel have the power to change cultural assumptions? Jesus approached people many times initially at the level of their temporal need. However, in pursuit of acknowledgment of their felt needs—which, by the way, was not a series he preached—Jesus told everyone in very short order the truth about his or her primary need. And that is where the entire felt needs emphasis in much of the seeker realm never seems to get off Dr. Phil's collective church couch.

If we were able to do so, it would be interesting to ask the rich young ruler who encountered Jesus if he felt any better about his felt needs when Jesus let him walk away after having told him what his real need was and how to have it met. In the same manner, the Samaritan woman at the well thought she needed water, a break from her lover, and a clarification on where to worship. But Jesus, after reading her mail, told her who he was and that the "water" she so desperately required was standing before her. Jesus ended up staying in Samaria a few days, and people got saved because they believed his own words. Jesus proclaimed who he was.

A Sovereign Visitation

Having recently reread *The Purpose-Driven Church*, I was reminded how Rick Warren used a great deal of the Scriptures in the assertions he was making. You may not agree with many of those assertions, or his interpretation of the Scriptures that led to those assertions, as many do not. And clearly, at a foundational level, I am reminded of how muted the gospel message really is. There are both positive and negative aspects as to how all those principles have played out in a broader context of seeker churches in general. I'm not suggesting an all-or-nothing approach.

On the heels of another Rick Warren book, *The Purpose-Driven Life*, however, and subsequent to the book's success, there has been a repeating theme of "trying God out," either as a way of establishing a relationship with him or in the co-development of plans for our purposes in life.

I readily acknowledge the wild popularity of these books. How can I argue with a zillion copies sold? Respectfully, however, there exists a potential for error when prescribing the God of all creation in forty-day regimens, or in the time it takes to form new habits. It is almost like someone could be trying to "just give God a shot," kind of like taking the Pepsi challenge. The predicament of unregenerate humanity is a bit weightier. I am also convinced Rick Warren is aware of that fact. He remains a worldwide and well-respected church influencer.

I also have a great deal of respect for Bill Hybels, who was an early pioneer of the large seeker-sensitive movement in the late 1970s with Willow Creek Church. At least he had the integrity to study his own premise and evaluate its effectiveness. It was found wanting, and the Willow staff have clearly communicated their problematic findings without a lot of spin. He and his leadership team have, in essence, found that money and emphasis into programs does not translate into spiritual growth and contentment.

Their study also indicated, if not empirically, then by experience, that those who were less centered in Christ were more satisfied with that church format. Why would it be otherwise? When you come to a church as an unbeliever and are not told much about the problematic nature of your spiritual status, there is not a whole lot of incentive for dramatic change; only change on the periphery seems called for. It is like the reality of "taking up your cross" becomes a *life skill* concept for doing all you can in life to do the right thing and be a good person. Jesus becomes the example for this way of living, a model for its attainment.

I do not believe the Willow Creek staff had that as either a motivation or even a distant thought. In fact, I am sure that in many cases they do not recognize their original mission from thirty years ago that is being played out now in many churches that have co-opted the seeker name. It is just what has evolved over the years in many seeker churches as the true gospel message has gotten pushed back further and further.

While I was an associate pastor at New Covenant Church in Knoxville, Tennessee, there was a period between 1992 and 1994 when we as a leadership team were really grappling with the whole issue of church growth, format, target audiences, and the like. We were becoming quite stagnant as a congregation. I was advocating many of the seeker principles at that time, not only because I felt they could set the course for our church, but also, honestly, those principles represented my own personal preference. We attended church growth seminars and confer-ences, and on one occasion Bill Hybels was a featured speaker. I found his vision and passion for communicating that vision very compelling. I was all for going forward with much of the seeker ministry as a church growth model.

Yet, what actually keyed the vitality of our church from the middle part of the 1990s and transformed it to doing what God had called us to do was not adopting precepts from the seeker model. Rather, it was a sovereign visitation by the Holy Spirit that started from a seed of repentance in the heart of our senior pastor.

I was fortunate enough to be a part of a renewal and revival that lasted for the better part of five years. Our church would never have been mistaken for the everyday seeker-sensitive church (which is the mother of all understatements). It was at that point that I began rethinking the entire church model. I came to believe that much of the contemporary church is like a postcard. There is the personal touch, it is inviting, and it elicits imagery. There is just enough visual and written information to form a mental portrait of some exotic destination. But it is only a small snapshot; it might highlight the best of a place, but it is not capable of revealing an accurate picture of the whole area. I think of the contemporary church in the same way. Looking at the church as a whole, it is a mixed bag. Some of its premise is unmistakably good. But so is eating a small portion of a chocolate cake. If I lived on it exclusively, however, I would turn into Jabba the Hutt.

Whatever impetus caused Hybels and Willow Creek to look critically at themselves, the fact that they did says much about the true intent of their hearts. One can only hope their message will begin to reflect the change to what they found was lacking. May God lead them by the Holy Spirit to do so, since they influence a huge portion of Christianity.

Made in the USA

The seeker churches have also tapped into the recognition of the value that postmoderns have placed in the cultural *ideal* of consumerism. Consumerism in the church is the idea that we are not only Christians, but we are *American Christians*. We have a keen sense of materialism. And even if we lack the self-awareness to know or admit it, we operate under three axioms of the postmodern age. First, we relish in our smorgasbord of seemingly unlimited choices. Second, we possess an overdeveloped sense of entitlement. And third, because of the first two reasons, we are independent souls who do not like being told what to do.

The entire seeker church ethos presumes and enhances our consumerism. In effect, both the seeker and the seeker church are creations of an interchangeable "cause and effect" relationship that forms this expression of the postmodern church. Like any smart consumer, seekers are only going to "buy" what they like. The seeker church, knowing the profile of the shopper, designs a product to meet the demand.

In recognition of the aforementioned three axioms, many seeker churches have begun advertising campaigns to tap into the "me-centered" proclivities of the age. One area where this is readily seen is with pastors pushing the idea of inviting folks "who are not religious" to churches, because they "don't like religion either." This is now a wildly popular notion. The media ads will declare, "At [So-and-So Nonreligious] Church, we aren't into rules, religion, or do's and don'ts." My favorite ad is, "If you're not into church or religion at all, you're going to love being with us on Sunday!"

We appeal to the "me-centered" generation because we think that to be religious is to be uptight, dogmatic, rigid, and incapable of having any fun. Worse yet, being religious is not wanting anyone else to have any fun! Or, you're living under the law and not acquainted with grace. I know this attitude is true because I have used it in a disparaging way to characterize people who I thought were rigid. In charismatic circles, it has been popular for years to establish your *bona fides* by spotting and declaring "religious" people, or "religious spirits."

In the broader context of the seeker churches, it is more of a buzzword to let the consumer know there will be no demands placed upon them, and little if any expectations to threaten either their independence or their range of choices. It is precisely this group of church consumers who need the true, uncompromised gospel boldly proclaimed in the clearest biblical context. The sad reality is that many are not hearing such a proclamation by many pastors because more temporal pursuits appear to be an easier row to plow.

You know how persnickety those consumers can be?

The purpose of the church is to proclaim the message of Jesus Christ as Savior and Lord, and to equip his disciples to proclaim that same message to others. Jesus came to "seek and save what was lost." The seeker, if truly cared for, must be loved enough to be told the truth of his eternal condition. His real issues are not relationships, career problems, or what to do with life in general. Rather, he is lost in his sin and can only be found, forgiven, and set free by the grace and power of Jesus Christ.

Perhaps we should inquire, "Who is seeking whom?"

May God's grace draw us to him where we will seek after him with all of our hearts.

Elvis Is Out in the Shack Listening to Miles Davis

Uh … thank you. Thank you very much.
—Elvis Presley

I WAS A college student living in Memphis and sitting in my apartment listening to WHBQ the afternoon Elvis died in August of 1977.

It was one of those surreal moments when the radio interrupted its normal broadcast with the grim news: "The king of rock 'n' roll is dead!" Being a history and philosophy major, it was not lost on me that this was not only a great cultural loss but a fairly important historical moment in our time. My roommate and I, sensing this was something we could tell our grandkids, talked about heading down to Graceland and joining the mass public response of shock and grief that was spontaneously occurring. We did not go at that time, but I planned on going the next day.

But the next day proved to be even crazier. Sometime in the early afternoon, a friend and I started out for Graceland, but it was clear from the radio reports we were not going to get within two miles of the place. We went back and read news reports saying the crowd estimates around Graceland ranged from a low of 50,000 to a high of over 100,000. It was wild! Not wanting to blow a good chance of impressing our grandchildren someday, we thought about parking and walking some distance. It was at that point that we realized a better tribute would be to turn the car around, go back to the apartment, fix some iced tea and peanut butter and banana sandwiches, and watch reruns of all the Elvis movies that began running twenty-four hours a day.

Besides, if I am blessed to be around when I am seventy-five years old, impressing my grandkids will fall in priority behind such things as remembering my own name and the premium I would surely be placing on managing risk by reminding myself not to buy any green bananas. That's what seven viewings of *Clam Bake* in one week will do to a young man. Not to mention that it was Memphis in August, when the oppressive heat is surpassed only by the even more oppressive humidity. I do remember reports of scores of people being treated for heat-related problems.

I also remember watching the TV reporting that week and being struck by the people of Memphis lining the streets and holding up pictures, albums, and homemade placards of Elvis from all stages of his career. People were everywhere. White, black, young and old, all paying tribute. It was quite amazing.

That week one could hear a number of tributes to Elvis, but there was one predominant theme that kept emerging. This theme was continually referred to by the news people as well as by the people the news people kept interviewing. It seemed that Elvis was a lot of things to a lot of people, but he was above all: the king of rock 'n' roll!

Who or What Was Elvis to You?

What does the recounting of that story have to do with postmodern truth and the church? Absolutely nothing, but I just thought you might be impressed since I still don't have grandchildren. But wait. Maybe on second thought this may have something to do with it, after all—especially the part where the various images of Elvis were everywhere, evoking different emotions and memories about "the King" from all those people lining the street.

Over and over reporters asked, "Sir, Madam, who or what was Elvis to you?" There were many different images and pictures, but almost without exception when all was said and done in describing who Elvis Presley was and what he meant to people, the almost unanimous reply was "Well, he was a lot of things, but if I had to boil it down to the one thing, he was *the king of rock 'n' roll.*"

It was darn near a consensus. Not scientific, but science does not matter when mourning icons. Most everyone who mourned the loss of Elvis was pretty much on the same page with their reflective assessment.

Rob Bell, a well-known Emergent leader and author of the popular book *Velvet Elvis*, maintains that there is no definitive portrait to describe Elvis, only attempts at interpreting him. The same can be said for Christianity. It too continues to be reinterpreted for the time in which we live. Bell is a compelling pastor who is engaging and well studied. He is an insightful man, which can be seen in any of his Nooma productions, short features that give application to biblical themes. In fact, I have used one of them specifically to teach in two different settings. I bring this up because even though I have written this book as if I had one minute to tell you everything important about postmodernism and the church, I do not wish to do a "drive-by" on those with whom I find areas of disagreement. Until late in 2007, I had recommended *Velvet Elvis* to many people who were asking questions about Christianity. I can no longer make such recommendations to that group of people, but I want to be clear as to why I consider Bell's book part of a troublesome trend in some of the Emergent movement. At the same time, I have to say that Bell's book does do a great job of reinforcing and encouraging believers in their pursuit of love and passion for Jesus.

Velvet Elvis

Velvet Elvis is one of the most important and popular Emergent Christian works of the last decade. It encapsulates the pretext for much of what is celebrated in the Emergent church movement. Chief among those objects of celebration are the things one does not know—the concept of *mystery*. The celebration of mystery eventuates in placing a high value on *questioning* in general, which, in turn, becomes a high type of virtue.

Bell speaks about the wonder of mystery in almost glowing terms of enlightenment. Take, for instance, his view of the Bible. And this is an area that became the cutting point for me, and why I have included this book in my examination. Asked in an interview about whether or not he had doubts regarding his previously held assumptions of the Bible, Rob (along with his wife, Kristen) admitted they rediscovered the Bible as a "human product rather than one of divine fiat." Rob continues: "The Bible is still the center for us, but quite a different center. We want to embrace mystery, rather than conquer it." "I grew up thinking that we've figured out the Bible," Kristen says, "that we knew what it means. Now I have no idea what most of it means. And yet I feel like life is big again—like life use to be in black and white, and now it's in color."[1]

To emphasize that these sentiments and new revelations regarding the Bible are not isolated, Rob continues in *Velvet Elvis*: "... insisting that one of the absolutes of the Christian faith must be a belief that 'Scripture alone is our guide.' It sounds nice, but it's not true."[2]

Oh, really? So it's not even *one* of the absolutes of the Christian faith? What else gets top billing?

It is evident, from a historical view of the Bible, that there is potential for some very serious problems with Rob Bell's position. I sadly sense a sort of giddy liberation that some of the more liberal wing of Emergents get from these types of assertions. It is like there is this sense of being emancipated from a Bible that does not work in the same way anymore because it cannot be understood. Somehow this uncertainty opens life up in Technicolor.

Writing in *Velvet Elvis*, Bell tells us that the point of embracing the mystery is that questions get raised that in turn help us to be "plunged into more questions," which demonstrates our inability to reach the deep mysteries of God. I would respectfully say that sounds like an overdeveloped sense of the prowess of mystery.

Besides, although I appreciate the fact that I will never figure God out, I am not overly enamored with being "plunged" into yet deeper levels of questions about God for which I am completely clueless. Call me simpleminded or too dogmatic; I just think life is better when it is possible to land on the surety of what the Bible does clearly say.

I will grant you the mystery. I wonder all the time how the sovereignty of God works. How does he orchestrate every moment of life for six billion people? But the greatest mystery to me is trying to grasp why God would send his Son to die for my sins. His love and forgiveness are unfathomable. It is a calculus I cannot grasp, and thinking about it leaves me in a state of awe and gratefulness. In that narrow context of mystery, one that elicits thanksgiving, I find myself agreeing that mystery provides great value in bringing me to my knees in awe of a good God.

That is why landing on the surety of the Bible concerning humankind is so amazing. As the apostle Paul says, "Now we have received, not the spirit of the world, but the Spirit who is from God, that we might *know* the things freely given to us by God" (1 Cor. 2:12). To what extent may we know them? We can know them to the extent our finite minds are submitted to the Sprit and we walk in the grace that comes from our faith in God and obedience to his Word. I don't claim to have all the answers. No, I don't even know most of the questions. But I believe God's Word concerning those things that it says the Holy Spirit will illuminate as I walk with him. I am totally dependent upon his enlightenment from his Word. And at best, in this life, you and I will only know in part. But we can know the foundational truths of our lives as believers and followers of Jesus Christ that enable us to live as overcomers, and as people of hope. Besides, one does not have to prove with metaphysical certitude that something is known to be true in order to believe that what is asserted to be true, is, in fact, true. The claims of the gospel are not only the external revelations of God to humans "by the Spirit," they also pass the evidentiary bar that is applied to the historical record. Empirically speaking, the claims of the gospel overwhelmingly pass the test that is applied to establishing the veracity of historical events. These include a prolific record of eyewitness, first-hand accounting; a consistent and time-tested record of documentation of gospel claims, as well as making these claims public, not private knowledge left to individual interpretation. For instance, Paul before Agrippa, or Peter at Pentecost appeal to the public knowledge of the claims of the gospels established years prior. Yet those claims had already become the public record of history—the external events that happened objectively in time and space concurred with and attested by scores of people. So even though I genuinely seek to move on cloaked in a garment of epistemic humility with my postmodern friends, the notion of proving something to be true with iron-clad certainty coexists peacefully with the grace given by the Holy Spirit to "know by the Spirit" those things for which you and I are convinced. We can "know" because God has given to us, by the Spirit, to know.

Reality and the Scriptures

Many in the postmodern church would probably refer to such a conviction as a need to feel secure, to which I would say, "You bet your mood candles it is!" I believe the Scripture calls it setting the feet upon a path that is lit by God's Word (Ps. 119:105). And I say that in full acknowledgment that while God is mysterious, "we have the mind of Christ" (1 Cor. 2:16b). Those two truths are not mutually exclusive, and we do not have to pick one or the other. They are complementary concurrent realities. What is troubling in Rob's assertion about the Bible is that his notion also chips away at the foundation of the historical assertion of *sola Scriptura* (that is, the idea that Scripture alone is our infallible authority), possibly rendering its status as dated as watching a VHS copy of *Viva Las Vegas*.

What makes this even more problematic is the compounding effect when pastors teach these things to others whom they influence, making the ground fertile for untold problems of Graceland proportions. The trouble Christians can get into with these types of "new conversations," which Emergents tell us are important, is that other people add their subjective perspectives to the discussion—because that quickly becomes the name of the game. And then there is a green light to saying and believing almost anything. Someone else takes the "conversation" a little further down the pike for more discussion and more nuance, and it gets further away from the fundamentals of the faith as proclaimed by Scripture. Clearly, it is not the discussion or questioning of aspects of our faith that is discouraged here. Not at all! Rather, the risk of error is derived from a pre-existent tendency to launch these discussions from an already watered-down origin of culturally-dependent sets of considerations drawn from interpretations from a culturally-determined bible. The next thing that happens is there may be the makings of another doctrinal or theological error, or worse.

When the communities, by asserting their special time and place in history, get to make subjective calls regarding the propositional truths of the Scriptures through individual interpretations as products of their *stories*, it may be a dynamic and exhilarating venture, but where does the plane land?

Before all this happens, if it has not already, I hope Rob Bell goes down the road a bit to reassess the status of where his initial insights have gotten him, insofar as influencing what people believe. He is one who influences many Christians and seekers who are curious about Christianity. He is a very passionate and thoughtful pastor, and I hope he reconsiders some of his initial postmodern assertions about the Bible.

But there is good news. Because of the stark contrast between what is true and what is mysterious, the celebrated truth-for-mystery trade gaining currency on the doctrinal playground of postmodernist Emergent churches provides an opportunity for the propositional truth of Scripture to be preached even more prolifically . This is done by countering the gospel of the unknown with the historical claims of the Bible.

For Bell in *Velvet Elvis*, when people look at the image of Elvis in the frame, it means different things to different people. It would not be fair or accurate for any individual to apply a universal truth to what appears in that frame, despite my slightly less-than-empirically-based "man-on-the-street" Memphis conclusion.

Donald Miller uses jazz music in *Blue Like Jazz* to underscore much the same theme as Bell. He points out that "Jazz doesn't resolve." And neither does God. For both of these authors the surety of being unsure becomes almost a cleansing agent or healing salve to be applied to the rigidness of an all-too-easy-to-explain but oversimplified orthodoxy—a Christianity that people generally cannot embrace without choking on it—or something that hardly anyone else would be attracted to.

Miller prefers you describe him less as a Christian and more as one who has accepted "Christian spirituality," even though he is not sure what that is. It is a very well-written personal journey about the premium given to the concepts of *contingency* and *skepticism,* both of which are high values of postmodernism. The only thing that hints of any propositional claim asserting any creedal tendency is Miller's obvious disdain for all things conservative, both politically and theologically. On that point he is not ambivalent. He is a terrific and thoughtful writer. The problem is that the reader could be left with the validation of *doubt* as a fixed and perpetual virtue, instead of serving as a vital transitory agent to objective conviction.

Both Miller's and Bell's books have helped crystallize the "orthodoxy" of the Emergent church, which ironically has become one of the most definitive expressions identifying cultural postmodernism as a whole.

He's in the Same Place I Am

I recommended both *Velvet Elvis* and *Blue Like Jazz* to many over the years—that is, until my own journey took a drastic turn and got rebooted. I suppose this shows the shallowness of my own convictions that I did not know particularly why I was recommending these books, outside of the fact that everyone was recommending these books. I liked edgy stuff because I believed that whatever *avant garde* notion that could draw the culture to Christ was a good thing, and so far as I was concerned, the end justified the means. Besides, the regular, everyday version of Christianity was rather boring. I was being very culturally relevant.

The trouble was that I did not use the Bible to evaluate how all that was working. And now I am completely convinced that what makes "regular" church boring and irrelevant is *not proclaiming* the biblical Jesus and his true gospel. It's not remedied by how cool we can make coming to church with a culturally relevant, but empty, message.

The last person I recommended the two books to was a man named Justin at the gym about four years ago. Justin is a fifty-year-old fitness freak who looks like a twenty-three-year-old male model. He's about 6' 2", with a washboard stomach, and without a pretentious bone in his ripped body. By contrast, I am a fifty-year-old with a body like a twenty-three-year-old pear, who looks in the mirror and comes away touting the virtue of a good personality. Justin is a brilliant man who is one of the most engaging, intelligent people I have ever met. We became friends just by talking casually while working out.

At some point early on, I told Justin I was a pastor at a Christian homeless and residential treatment ministry, and he told me he was at a point in his life that he was really trying to figure out the whole "Christianity thing." He said he had never been a believer but that he was going to church every week, listening to teaching, going to Bible classes, and really taking an analytical approach to coming to terms with the validity of Christianity for his life.

We would talk about the Bible and I would try encouraging him, but he had a thousand questions. I tried to answer every one. Obviously I was not able to answer all his questions, and I was okay with that fact. And when I would answer, our conversation would often morph into a circular logic of more and more questions that were unanswerable. But this just validated another case in point for not letting witnessing for Christ turn into intellectual banter instead of at some point directing the conversation to law and grace.

Don't get me wrong. I loved being Justin's friend, but I was still at a point in my pastoral journey where, sadly, I generally did not witness to people through their real need. I usually subscribed to the strategy of *winning over the long haul* with my life before them as the primary teacher. So for Justin, as with others during this time, I recommended *Velvet Elvis* and *Blue Like Jazz*.

Justin read some reviews on Bell's book and decided to pass, but he did begin to read *Blue Like Jazz*. He came back to me and basically related that it was okay and that "this guy sounds like he's in the same place that I am." When I asked him what he meant, he said that Miller seemed to be trying to find answers but coming away with more questions. So Justin said he did not actually finish the book.

I deeply regret not having directly shared the true gospel at some point with my friend. Sometime before I moved away, Justin began traveling quite a bit, and we had not seen each other for several months before my family moved across the country. My hope and prayer is that Justin is born again. I hope my time with him at least planted some good seeds so that someone else could come along and water the seeds. I believe without a shadow of a doubt that he was being drawn to the Lord by the Holy Spirit.

Emerging Issues

Toleration, celebration,
Let's make it clear, we don't want no rigid dogma here.
Proclamation Abdication—next thing you know, you got—
No gospel nation

—Postmodern Hymn #915

I love being around many Emergent Christians because of what they bring to worship and because of their reinvigorating approach to of aspects of liturgy. Tony Jones, a prolific Emergent leader and writer, refers to the engaging of our senses in worship to help us experience the "transcendence of God." I completely concur because I think engaging our senses helps us bring our whole being into worshiping the Lord, which Scripture encourages believers to do. I have been to Emergent churches and, other than needing a flashlight to get to my seat, I really appreciated their holistic, expressive approach to worship, including emphasis upon the arts.

If you go to the unofficial official Web site of the Emergents, "The Ooze" (www.theooze.com), you get a fascinating look at the postmodern tenets and orthodoxy. It is a virtual celebration of *skepticism, doubt,* and everyone *rethinking something.* It is such a mirror of what is going on the larger culture that one could make a claim that the Emergents are a major catalyst for defining the totality of the cultural era in which we live.

Emergents have developed an entire lexicon to identify those in their movement. For example, one hears a lot about "in the way of Jesus," "community," "new conversations," "story," the freedom found in "skepticism," and the quest for life and mystery that is found in the splendor of "questions." Yet, one of their highest stated values remains *authenticity.* That is an extremely interesting juxtaposition by Emergents, given that the word *authenticity* is derived from the ideal of what is authoritative and reliable—believable, as it were. It is an interesting irony.

Another emphasis among Emergents is the problematic notion of dualistic thinking. That is why *A Generous Orthodoxy,* the book by Emergent leader Brian McLaren, is not about the author having an identity crisis on the front cover of his book. Rather, its subtitle *Dualisms* is there to highlight the pitfalls of dualistic thinking. To pit one view against the other forces an undesirable outcome of landing the plane on an actual belief runway. It is too simplistic, without a multitude of filters. That is why McLaren suggests he can, for instance, be Methodist and Catholic at the same time. His own story of crisis in his journey as a believer is very compelling, and I find myself agreeing with many things he asserts regarding the value of living our faith in the community of believers. His call for Christians to pursue both the wonder and awe of God is a wonderful theme. But I find many of his doctrinal assertions troubling, especially those related to the atonement and his view of the cross, just to name a couple. He is probably the leading voice of the uber-Emergents, although he insists he does not preside over a "movement." He would describe it more as a "conversation."

Emergents also emphasize "missional living," a kind of Christianity-by-social-activism, which fits nicely into their stress of the "here and now," as opposed to an archaic traditional creed that has defined heaven and hell (a dualism) as hard target destinations of an incentive-based religion that either rewards or punishes in the future. Emergent thinking suggests the planet and its people are all redeemable through activism by the community *in the way of Jesus*, which forms strategies to create an earth that Jesus would be proud of—and perhaps one he would desire to come back to.

The net result of this sort of neo-post-Woodstock millen-nialism, however, can look very similar to righteousness by works—which, ironically, is what many Emergents say they detest about many of the conventions of traditional Christianity. The "community" has to get on the ball and do good things, because what we have been given is all worth saving. It's not always doing good *because* we have come to know Christ, but it can border at times on good works so that we *can* know Christ.

But who is going to blow the horn to say enough is enough? How do we know when we have filled the quota of good deeds on earth so that God deems us a worthy partner in the pursuit to jumpstart everyone's divine spark? A system of works without the gospel renders us desperate in the end, because salvation depends not on the good works we do but on what Jesus has done and continues to do in our lives through forgiveness and atonement. This is the divine means of grace, and it is from that point of our faith in him that good works will flow.

What if the Big One Comes?

There is a profound reason why elevating the status of mystery and the preoccupation with questioning the orthodox truth claims of Christianity are causes for concern. And it has to do with the times we have entered. A faithful life is going to be tested. It will be as a shaking and sifting. What is going to be the likely response when the heat of persecution is turned up in our culture, as it surely will, specifically targeting Christianity as an institution and Christians as individuals? In other words, if you have set your faith on uncertainty and mystery, and you have resolved that questions provide a more exciting way to live than standing on faithful answers, what will you cling to when you suffer unjustly?

How are you likely to endure such pressure and trial? What would compel you to want to endure? How far will the gospel of uncertainty go in providing a resolve and faith to live out Christianity in the face of ridicule, let alone real persecution, when shades of gray will no longer be an option? How long is mystery and skepticism, even in the context of a tightly knit community, going to sustain you when the stuff hits the fan? If it's unclear what I stand upon, how can I, "having done everything to stand," tie myself to the mast of … what? That's why I am glad authenticity is a stated high value with Emergents, because only an unqualified authentic faith will sustain any of us when faced with persecution—as surely those days come rapidly toward us.

The Bible speaks of a major portion of people falling away (apostasy) as times of peril increase. And consider this: What if the trouble and dark times are not a direct attack of persecution by the secular forces of the culture but are things like natural calamity and widespread disaster that inflict great physical, financial, and emotional loss in one's life? I fear there will be many "Christians" and false converts from every stream of

Christianity who will shake their fists and curse God because this is not what they were told was going to happen by following their version of Jesus and his gospel.

Jesus spoke of the importance of the kind of foundation a house is built upon. He warned us not to be "like a foolish man who built his house on sand. The rain came down, the streams rose, and the winds blew and beat against that house, and it fell with a great crash" (Matt. 7:26–27 NIV). He used that analogy to warn us that great times of storm and peril are coming. And they are coming even in America. Only one foundation will hold.

Mac's Got a Visitor—or Three

Another book that has found enormous popularity in all streams of postmodern Christianity is *The Shack*, by William P. Young. This is another extremely well-written book that does what any great novel does: It transports readers by its imagery and its ability to get them emotionally involved. *The Shack* was another book I often recommended. I even handed it to my daughter as she boarded a plane for a six-month YWAM mission to Northern Ireland.

Way to go, Dad!

As much as I initially liked it, I had a sense that something was off the track when coming to the part of the encounter with Young's modalistic trinity. That is the doctrine that the Holy Spirit can have many interchangeable modes of identity, as opposed to the historical biblical view of one God in three distinct persons. Many have criticized *The Shack* due to its hints of universalism through Young's Jesus character's self-description: "I will travel any road to find you" and "Those who love me come from every system that exists." Then there is its treatment of the second commandment.

I have said many times to many friends that I am aware we are no longer under the law. However, it would be beyond

91

stupid for me as a believer to willingly break one of God's Ten Commandments on the basis that I am no longer bound by it. I would apply that first to the other six-hundred—plus Old Testament laws before I would the Ten Commandments. Why in the name of Charlton Heston would anyone want to knowingly break one of the Ten Commandments as proof they are free from it—assuming they are?

Our freedom from the law means Jesus' life and death has, by faith, sufficiently fulfilled our obligation of its perfect completion. Short of that atonement, one lustful thought from me would brand me "guilty" as an adulterer. Thank God for his grace.

I am also not accusing Young of knowingly advocating breaking God's commandments. I am just talking about the net result in discerning the merits of something claiming to be biblical by so many people, by actually using the Bible to do that very thing. When I bring up the doctrinal problems with Young's story to my friends, I get what I call the "*Oh God* pass." I have been one of its proponents. The *Oh God* pass came when I was enjoying George Burns (another depiction of god) in the movie *Oh God* in the late 1970s, right up to the point he tells John Denver that Jesus was one of many sons of various world religions that were his, including Buddha and Mohammad. So I said, "Yeah, that part was troubling, but it was a great movie, and it may get people turned on to God, so I'll give it a qualified pass."

I loved George Burns in that movie, but I do not recall a revival breaking out after it hit the screen. Meanwhile, as interest in anything spiritual from the culture explodes in growth, there have been Web sites devoted to whether Tolkien's Gandalf of *The Lord of the Rings* is a type of the Holy Spirit, Moses, Michael the archangel, Jesus, or Winston Churchill. I am personally convinced he is a type and shadow of Howie Mandel. But we continue to seek spiritual meaning and message in the context of arts, entertainment, and the culture at large. We crave its pursuit, while relishing any hint as a hopeful significance for our lives. What a time to proclaim the gospel!

For the record, I think the Trinity is one of the most amazing mysteries in all of Christianity. And so is the mystery of the *kenosis*: what went on when Jesus "emptied himself" and took on the form of a man? How does it work that Jesus is 100 percent God and 100 percent man at the same time? Rob Bell calls these doctrines "springs" that help believers get a good bounce on the trampoline of their relationship with God. What a great analogy! He recommends we take the springs out and "bend" them—examine them and inspect how they work—because they are strong and we are not going to break them by inspection. Again, that is a reasonable proposal that could serve to strengthen the faith of believers.

But here's the rub, Rob. Let's take the doctrine of hell. When that "spring" becomes so bended that it can no longer support any more than a *slinky*, you could end up claiming that hell is little more than a metaphor for such things as "famine," "debt," and "oppression," all of which Rob concludes are things that cause "hell on earth." No doubt they do. And certainly these calamities could mimic types and shadows of an eternal hell, understated as they are. But the question becomes, "Does the metaphor for hell replace what the Bible calls a specific destination of hell, which was created for the Devil and his angels, and where actual unredeemed people are going to spend all eternity?"

Because if hell is a just a metaphor for the awful things on the planet, then the gospel message is compromised. The Woodstock version of the gospel is kept intact, but as far as the true gospel goes, the slinky breaks, and you might just bruise your spiritual coccyx when falling though the weakened trampoline and landing on the pavement.

Proclaim the true gospel, my Emergent friends, even while we are inspecting the springs. It's great that they are not mutually exclusive endeavors.

There are wonderful mysteries in Christianity. Yet Christianity's power is derived from what is true—and that is God's Word—his faithful Word, and his gospel message, which transcends the times and the culture in which we live. The great mystery of God is revealed to us in the appearance of the Savior and Redeemer, Jesus Christ. It is in him that all mystery finds its culmination and resolution. God has indeed spoken. "And the rest," as succinctly put by Rob Bell, "is commentary, right?"

One final note: as we go to print with Postcards, reviews abound regarding Bell's new book entitled, *Love Wins: A Book about Heaven, Hell, and the Fate of Every Person Who Ever Lived.* Judging by what I have read in the reviews, it looks like the metaphorical hell of *Velvet Elvis* just got an upgrade. And just like the literal Elvis, the literal hell has apparently left the building (hopefully not with Elvis)! I'm personally pulling for you Rob—that somehow the reviews I've read are merely the assessments of many who are just narrow-minded purveyors of foundationalism. What do they have to offer except two-thousand years of settled Church doctrine on the subject? That's only their opinion.

I hope if you're asking us to "rethink" heaven and hell (and I'm betting two passes to Graceland you are), that some of us may read the book, and respectfully decline the offer. Besides, I've already been to Graceland. Or perhaps we'll demonstrate a more tolerable open-mindedness by actually rethinking our positions regarding these eternal destinations, only to conclude that the literal heaven is far more blissful and exciting than we first thought; and the literal hell is infinitely more terrible than we had originally conceived. Most importantly, may Jesus Christ, whether of faith in him by his disciples, or disdain of him by his enemies be recognized and exalted as king and authority—the arbiter of eternity. It's my prayer that the Holy Spirit will quicken the hearts and minds of people to the wonder of that truth.

Twenty-Somethings Just for You; Social Justice Under Review

Ecumenical man, social justice is my plan-
And that's about as doctrinaire;
Unless of course, you want to talk... Clean Air?
Then I'm downright expository—
Wanna know the Greek for carbon footprint?

—Postmodern Hymn #915

THERE IS NO group of people who are in general more passionate and more engaging than twenty-somethings. I absolutely marvel at their incredible zeal for life, their collective adventuresome spirit, and their commitment and dedication for causes to which they are drawn. These are qualities those of us who are older would do well to emulate. One thing is for sure: the twenty-somethings are intense!

Those characteristics are even more amplified when you see them played out in the lives of twenty-something believers. I have seen the same dynamic all over the world, where I have been privileged to meet many twenty-somethings in different countries and from different cultures. What I notice almost immediately is that they share this common thread of giving their all and going to the wall for what they believe. They are amazing!

I suppose it has always been like that with young adults, perhaps in every time period in every culture. Although I have to say that when I was twenty-one the thought of getting "turned on" by the prospect of going to China for four months to smuggle Bibles to the underground church was not readily available on my radar screen.

Actually, my limit for daring at twenty-one was two days in the Smoky Mountains (one night actually camping and two days in the park, so technically two days) camping next to the ranger station with showers, vending machines, and a ranger who would tuck me in at night (on the couch of the lobby at the station) and leave the floodlights on. They had a bear problem … a really huge one!

But I am completely blown away by how twenty-somethings answer the call of God in their lives, how they like to spend their summers and take off semesters in college to go to Africa, Southeast Asia, Eastern Europe, or the inner cities of the USA to serve and minister. I know many of them, and I have watched them grow up and leave home to attend ministry schools and take extended mission trips. I have seen them get involved in prayer ministries, where they go from three months to three years to do intercessory prayer and worship all day or all through the night.

Dude, It's Social Justice!

Being around twenty-somethings energizes me, and I love to hear them talk about what they are "into" as far as ministry is concerned. They recognize that their destiny is being forged in front of them day by day. There is no cause that is any hotter among twenty-somethings in the culture as a whole, as well as among the Christian twenty-somethings of the church, than the cause of social justice. It is red hot—*en fuego*! It is hot at their colleges and at their college and career groups at church. Interest in social justice is all over their favorite media and entertainment venues, and it is the focal point of coffee conversations at their favorite cafes. To borrow an expression from another generation of twenty-somethings, social justice is in, man!

And, dude, why not? Who is not for social justice? Opposing social justice would be like saying you are not for green grass in the spring, lemonade on a hot summer day, or that Christmas should be canceled this year. What's not to be for? Social justice is a hot topic within in every demographic of the postmodern church, but this is especially true of the twenty-somethings.

I certainly do not want to disparage interest in social justice. But I want to suggest that, as believers, it is good to know *why* we are involved in so many things that come under its rubric. Social justice is a growing concept in the church and is being absorbed into the mainstream of Christianity. This causes me to pause and look at why it has gained such cultural prominence. It is not new, of course. It has been around in American society for well over one hundred years, but it sure garners lots of conversation from those who advocate it is the Lord's work—as well as those who do not.

What actually is this social justice, and why is it so important to embrace as a Christian? It has political, social, and religious implications, and Christians want to know which side of the issue everyone is on. It is clear from the Bible that true social justice is a mandate from God. The only question is, What kind of mandate?

I am in my eleventh consecutive year of ministry directly focusing upon the homeless, the abused, the addicted, and the poor. While that does not necessarily qualify me as an expert on social justice, I would like to believe I have earned some "skin in the game" when it comes to discussing this controversial topic. To the extent I have built any capital on the issue, I will spend it here. Within the context of the postmodern church, social justice themes many times will center on the ethics of Jesus, while remaining eerily silent about his mission of the cross and resurrection for the sacrificial payment of our sin. Indeed his status is often undifferentiated from any other revolutionary who comes to shake up the conventions of society.

I am compelled to open this can of worms because of my concern that those who burn with a passion for God's social justice mandate understand that such work is always a *work of grace* and not a humanistic work. If it is a work that derives from only human interest, it is just another form of self-righteous legalism. Indeed, herein lies the whole debate: Can social justice be a true type of social justice if it is not biblically mandated social justice?

"I Do not Think it Means what You Think it Means"

On its face, the term itself has a very positive connotation that automatically gives its advocate a kind of moral edge—a built-in advantage. Those concerned for social justice seem to get an automatic pass for having feelings and compassion for political, social, and religious issues. Like protected speech, it is not PC to speak of it in anything but glowing terms. The sanitizing value of the term itself may be a reason why so many organizations have social justice as their mission. At the very least, it is hard not to notice that it can produce some very strange bedfellows.

What seems to be happening to a great degree is the large-scale co-opting of the term *social justice*, so that it carries a host of meanings and connotations depending upon the agenda of the organization. Clearly, it is not a one-size-fits-all meaning. To quote the famous Spaniard swordsman and part-time philosopher, Inigo Montoya: "I do not think it means what you think it means."

That is true, and even among Christians the meaning of social justice differs. Who can debate that we have an obligation to the poor, the widow, the orphan, the oppressed, and the marginalized? In the book of James, we are told that caring for these is the definition of "true religion." And the prophet Isaiah speaks of justice for the oppressed. No one can read the Bible and doubt God's heart for the oppressed and the poor—and what God expects the believer's posture toward them to be.

Feeding people who are hungry, clothing those who are naked, providing shelter for those who are unprotected, and advocating for those who have little or no access shows us what we should understand about the heart of the Lord. It is the most fundamental way we love people. But it is not necessarily social justice, at least as prescribed by secularists.

Feeding, clothing, and protecting the less fortunate are commanded by Scripture for believers to embrace, but they are to be done without any agenda other than basic Christian charity. In other words, I give food to the hungry if they need food because they need food. And as a Christian, I do so in the name of Jesus. It is not the same when getting into anti-poverty campaigns, or labor, job, housing, and education issues. (I have actually seen social justice signs where students were protesting proposed college tuition hikes.) Those issues entail institutional objectives and involve government, politics, unions, special interest groups, businesses, and so on. Christians need to understand that such causes are governed by these institutional interests, so we better be able to delineate the specifics of what we are championing, and under whose banner we are proceeding. In the meantime, isn't it odd that you rarely see social justice coupled with issues regarding justice for the unborn?

Social justice is often the centerpiece of particularly very radical organizations. Accordingly, they may feature very interesting Web sites that automatically become more mainstreamed when, regardless of the radical nature of their political and societal aims, *social justice* is included. It softens the sale. As a result, the current popularity of the term in the culture lends credibility to organizations espousing everything from anarchy to Marxism, from social gospel to socialism, and from communism to Christianity.

I am concerned about associations and causes as they relate to biblical mandates for Christians. My point in bringing them up is to show the wide variance of what seems to be a broad use of the term and to suggest that there is a historical association of the term with many organizations and political philosophies that may prompt us to look closer. Are Christians talking about the same social justice as anarchists? It appears that social justice in the abstract makes strange bedfellows, as would be the case if Simon Cowell or Ozzy Osborne opened a chain of charm schools. They are nice enough fellows, but would you readily associate them with "Miss Manners?"

The Greater Grace

What is true social justice and what should our response to it be as believers? What it is not is a catch-all for things done by Christians who automatically assume it is a "Jesus thing." We have to be clear about social justice because if it is not done by the believer from a motivation of the *gospel* of Jesus, and not just the *ethics* of Jesus, then the believer who has been freed from the law could slip back to the law of works in an effort to do what Martin Luther calls "satisfying the external demands of the law."

Without the gospel of Jesus, when will we have done enough to merit the righteousness of God? How will we know? The work of social justice may be very good work, if one doesn't presume one is reconciled to God by it. By that I mean we are not to help the poor because Jesus did that, but we should help them because Jesus himself through the power of his gospel can break the bondage of the poverty of the soul. This should be the point in all the work of social justice we do while addressing the physical and temporal needs of the poor and oppressed.

The reality of groups holding a claim in the cause of social justice, who also hold so many different agendas, should be a signal for us to examine carefully how the Christian perspective differs from all other perspectives or approaches to the causes and remedies of social justice. And here is the first problem with embracing all things social justice. Particularly in the contemporary American version, advocates have demanded remedy on behalf of causes under the banner of social justice, when in reality they are really demanding social *fairness*. Social justice and social fairness is a distinction with a huge difference. The Bible is clear about the mandate for us to advocate, and proactively influence, the "just" treatment of the poor and downtrodden. This means that we are to support on their behalf justice in the sense of access to all of society's doors.

What cannot be guaranteed by the society, and what is not mandated in the Scriptures, are *equal outcomes*, which are a feature of social fairness, or even socialism. This is not biblical social justice. Quite the contrary. For instance, people are obviously born into families of different socioeconomic conditions. Some are very rich, some are very poor, and some are scattered all over the scale.

We cannot overstate the role of the ravages of sin in all this. Poverty and injustice are ultimately fruits of the fallen human condition. We are all perpetrators, and we are all victims, because we have all sinned. Sin is a universal reality that transcends economic scales. It is an equal opportunity destroyer. And the Scriptures make it clear that there is no distinction between the rich and the poor as it relates to the justice of God, because the scales of a just God are balanced perfectly before all—regardless of economic status.

There is a vast difference between *justice,* which is derived from God, and *fairness,* which is a human invention that we sometimes confuse with justice. Here is an example. Eric Clapton is a phenomenal guitar player. I enjoy playing the guitar, but I am only average as far as skill and talent level. If I practiced every day for one hundred years, while Clapton slept, I still would not come close to playing the way he does. (I am thoroughly convinced that if *he* practiced for one hundred years he would not be able to top himself!) My assessment of the situation is an absolute statement of a truth to which my guitar-playing postmodern friends could agree.

I could stomp my feet and cry, "That's not fair!" And it is not fair that Clapton is a better guitar player than I am or will ever hope to be. Of course it's not fair. But it is a completely *just* outcome for a number of reasons. God gave Eric Clapton innate talent and ability for that specific skill that he did not give me (which is, by the way, not fair). I also refused to put in the effort early on to perfect the limited ability that I did have, like Clapton did. Music was a higher priority of interest and pursuit for him than it has ever been for me. In the final analysis, he just has the chops, and I do not. Many things in life are unfair, but they are nevertheless just. Trying to equalize the outcome to this problem may make me feel better about your concern for me, but the universe of guitar-playing quality is going to suffer dramatically if you give me the same top billing as Clapton. He may as well go play the tuba.

The distinction between justness and fairness must be acknowledged or we can get into "righting" all the "wrongs" of society based upon a misplaced motivation of fairness. And how much do you really want, in the name of fairness, to hear *Bell Bottom Blues* played on the tuba? I know this is a silly example, but it's not far off in describing what many people demand in social justice.

Furthermore, when the apostle Paul gave instructions to help widows, there were guidelines set for who qualified for what. For example, if a woman was over sixty years old but had someone in the immediate or extended family who could care for her, she was not eligible for help. But a woman of the same age who had no one to care for her was granted relief. Is that fair? They were both widowed and over sixty. That seems a little harsh, does it not? I mean, that is quite a generalization the apostle is making there. What about the nuance of someone's special situation? Wish we could get Paul on Larry King to defend that.

It is corrupt human processes that create the corrupt institutions that shackle people who are wrongly oppressed, and this is what must be justly amended to give the poor equal access to those institutions, whether they be economic, civil, medical, educational, or what have you. What I am sure we cannot do is dictate that outcomes must be distributed equally over the whole of society. There are far too many other variables that enter into the equation.

In America, Christians who call for the government to right all the wrongs of society need to remember that it is that very government that has begun curtailing the liberties of Christians related to public expressions of faith. The government giveth; the government taketh away!

I am not an anarchist or a militia member (I am not even a Republican), but I know that real corruption starts when government and political forces at any level want to "do good," as defined by their agenda. They always do it at the expense of someone else. That is not social justice; that is social engineering. Providing a safety net for the most vulnerable is one thing, but a government picking causes as it sees fit is quite another. By contrast, overseas, where ten-year-old girls are sold into the sex-slave industry, all bets are off. Providing rescue may mean interacting with very corrupt governments is unavoidable in transacting deliverance for these precious children. Social justice

103

is a whole different ball game in these countries than in America because the issues and advocacies are stark in contrast. In third world countries, ministries are involved in literal life and death issues for the oppressed. In the States, we readily attach social justice to various political causes, as can be read on placards at almost any rally in protest of most any issue.

The current Pope Benedict has described political institutions that desire to do God's work as anything but divine. In fact, he calls their designs "demonic." Governments would do well to provide the incentives, or at least get out of the way for nonprofits, private charities, and churches to do the work that historically they have done much better than government.

We Are the World

There are ecumenical movements among very progressive churches that now trumpet themselves as *anti-poverty* coalitions *working with others* in the name of social justice. When I hear such a description, three questions immediately come to my mind. The first is, "Where are the pro-poverty churches?" I have got to see these people, religious or otherwise, who advocate the proliferation of poverty. Who are they? Maybe we can turn Geraldo Rivera on them. I want to hear their mission statement, and I want to know how they sleep at night.

The second question is, "Can you tell me a little about the *others* you are working with?" I ask that now because too often the true gospel message of Jesus gets compromised in the name of ecumenical unity. Sometimes the true gospel message gets thrown under the bus.

And the third question is, "What is the endgame?" This is the really important question because it reveals both the group's mission and motivation. Where is Jesus, and how is he depicted? Is he presented exclusively as the concerned, socially conscious icon, or is he Savior and Lord? Are we co-opting his name for our causes?

The Divine Spark Needs a New Set of Jumper Cables

When this issue of justice and fairness stays murky, a quest for social justice can become a social justice motivated by a *social gospel*. Of course that time-honored institution has ebbed and flowed in the U.S. since the turn of the twentieth century. There are two tenets that help to describe the social gospel. One is the premise of applying Christian principles to solve society's problems created by the industrialization of America in and around 1900. The sentiment was that when Jesus said, "Love thy neighbor," that meant to the social gospel proponents that there needed to be a whole host of programs designed to address the problems created by the society, reflecting that love and concern.

That thought led to the other tenet, which is that the issue of *sin* should be looked at as a collective societal problem rather than the responsibility of the individual. Therefore to a large degree, the individual's predicament is society's fault and society's responsibility. Even if that is not directly espoused, it is the effective belief by which many social gospel advocates operate.

And that is where the social gospel train jumps the track.

If society is the exclusive sinner, then all the problems and their extinction become the focus, and those social problems become causes that keep morphing into sub-causes. When that happens, the human problem of sin gets eclipsed by every other societal and political initiative, from housing and healthcare to global warming. After all, that is surely what God wants, right?

Who is evaluating all this and what standard are they using to make judgments and conclusions? Is it the Bible or a political agenda, someone's preferred worldview or the Comedy Central channel?

Nevertheless, the identification and solution to social problems remains a powerful assertion for many who ascribe to the ethics of Jesus in addressing problems in the culture. To the social gospel advocate, the prevailing belief is that if you remove all the negative conditions that have shackled him, man's divine spark will be liberated to become all he was meant to be.

The train that earlier jumped the tracks just went over the side of the cliff!

The human condition of being mired in sin is not the only issue. It is that our sin has rendered us *spiritually dead*. And that is deader than trying to jump-start a '69 chartreuse VW van in February from North Dakota that hasn't been started since the Jesus movement. If you tried jumping it with a small nuclear reactor, you wouldn't get a peep out of it. Yet the proponent of a vague social gospel sees humans as inherently good. If society provides the right tools, our good nature will bloom like a blue-ribbon rose at the state fair. That is a great thought and a noble and caring view of human beings, but from the perspective of Scripture, it is a completely inaccurate and erroneous view.

God created us in his own image. Therefore, we are intrinsically of great, great *value,* more valuable than anything else in his creation. This does not make us intrinsically good, however, and we could not be good intrinsically if we wanted to. The reason for this is that the human nature is sinful by our breaking the law of a holy God, and by qualification of birth through the sin curse of Adam. "Therefore, just as sin entered the world through one man, and death through sin, and in this way death came to all men, because all sinned" (Rom. 5:12 NIV).

We are born with a sense that there is a God, which we can readily see in the whole of creation. Our course of life is set, whether we acknowledge and glorify God or suppress the truth about him. The apostle Paul wrote,

For the wrath of God is revealed from heaven against all ungodliness and unrighteousness of men, who suppress the truth in unrighteousness, because what may be known of God is manifest in them, for God has shown it to them. For since the creation of the world His invisible attributes are clearly seen, being understood by the things that are made, even His eternal power and Godhead, so that they are without excuse, because, although they knew God, they did not glorify Him as God, nor were thankful, but became futile in their thoughts, and their foolish hearts were darkened.

—Rom. 1:18–21

If we continue to suppress the truth about God, we will seal our condemnation, which will put us in a worse position than finding out we were not intrinsically good in the first place. And that is a whole lot worse than bad housing and having a bad landlord who refuses to take care of the plumbing.

Of course, any status of "goodness" is attained only through the righteousness of Jesus, which is impossible for people to merit, and which is why we need a Savior.

Kingdom Social Justice: A Grace-empowered "Work"

At the beginning of the church, right after Pentecost, there was such an outpouring of care and support for believers in Jerusalem that the needs of people were being met in this amazing orchestration of the Holy Spirit working through the new Christians.

This is recounted for us in the fourth chapter of the book of Acts:

Now the multitude of those who believed were of one heart and one soul; neither did anyone say that any of the things he possessed was his own, but they had all things in common. And with great power the apostles gave witness to the resurrection for the Lord Jesus. And great grace was upon them all. Nor was there anyone among them who lacked; for all who were possessors of lands or houses sold them, and brought the proceeds of the things what were sold, and laid them at the apostles' feet; and they distributed to each as anyone had need.

—Acts 4:32–35

This is a passage of Scripture that reveals so much about the spirit, purpose, and motivation of a community of believers who demonstrated to the world the love and power of Jesus Christ in those early days. It is the basis for true biblical social justice, and it is still a model for addressing similar problems today.

Acts 4:32–35 is not a picture of a quaint little Euro-socialist utopia where life was grand and everyone was given his or her fifteen weeks off each year to holiday on the Riviera. Neither was it a compulsory grab of someone else's resources to demonstrate the collective harmony of the involuntary redistribution of wealth.

Looking very closely at what is happening in this passage reveals why this is so amazing. The passage says they were "of one heart and one soul." What was the unifying agent that had them express such oneness? What made them so united? The next sentence gives us the clear answer: They "gave witness to the resurrection of the Lord Jesus." It was the reality and power of the resurrected Savior through an outpouring of the Holy Spirit that caused this amazing coalescence of purpose.

The passage also says that "great grace was upon them all." It was this "great grace" upon them that created a heart for people of means to go sell their possessions and care for those in need. It was not a works orientation with some esoteric goal of making the earth a better place. It was not accomplished by directing the people to redistribute their wealth if they wanted to be considered good Christians.

No, what made the early Christians so united was the supernatural spiritual outworking of *grace* that came through their hope of the *resurrection of Christ*. This was the object of and the reason for their action. And it served as a great witness to the world as to how the poor and downtrodden could be ministered to in the name of Jesus Christ, the resurrected Savior and Lord.

Jesus himself *is the cause and motivation* for true social justice for believers. Anything else risks a works-merit system that has so many more attachments that can be self-serving, self-righteous, and laced with motivations that have claims of God but have more to do with elevating the status of people and their deeds, politics, and worldviews. That is how you end up with the T-shirt franchise featuring the split screen of Che Guevara and Jesus.

A rose by any other name still smells like a salvation by works.

As the church, we must administer social justice with all the passion and purpose for which we have been called, but we must also take the cause of social justice in the name of Jesus and his gospel. We are to go in his name and proclaim *him*. We feed the poor not only because Jesus told us to do that, but also because *he is their life and their hope*. This demonstrates the power and love of Jesus Christ and is the work of divine grace that is the underlying principle for true biblical social justice.

Jesus is the centerpiece, not an organization with a political cause. There are just too many other things attached to political causes. And with governments come too many strings that can be broken and too many alliances that have the effect of turning the church from its mission into an arm of an unyielding government yoke that changes according to political tides.

True social justice is a call of the church. By the Holy Spirit, let us use good judgment to dispense good social justice.

There are a number of Christian organizations that are doing the Lord's work in the cause of social justice around the world. I can offer no higher endorsement for involvement with a Christ-centered social justice organization than can be conferred to Wesley and Stacy Campbell's organization, Be a Hero. They take the banner of the gospel to minister to children in poverty, homelessness, the sex-slave industry, those in the plagues and ruins of war, and many more causes. I encourage you to visit their Web site at www.Beahero.org. I also readily endorse Operation Blessing International, www.Ob.org, as well as www.worldvision.org. Both are international organizations with whom I have firsthand knowledge and experience of their ministry around the world in addressing the causes of poverty and injustice from a Christ-centered perspective.

A Postcard from the Hangar: The King Air 200 Is Blowin' Oil!

TODAY'S VERSION OF prosperity preachers bears little resemblance to their forerunners from a generation ago. The modern installment features such effective market-savvy messaging that the Christian motivational speaker and life-success circuit has, in many ways, eclipsed the secular guru's success. There is now an entire industry that has gone darn near mainstream. Many of them can go toe-to-toe with Tony Robbins, and any other secular guru, in the ability to create and capture the "good life" market. And their messages have proven to have crossover appeal to many non-Christians. These folks are good. As they reference God on occasion, often the context is so amazingly world-friendly that no nonbeliever in the house could dare get offended, unless they were just looking for something to dislike.

Some of these speakers do mention Jesus quite often, but they have an amazing ability to take a passage of Scripture concerning Jesus, or even one of his parables, and form the most interesting and improbable interpretations. This would include asserting the spiritual benefit of shopping, or the importance of acquiring brand names as a way to ensure that God does not get relegated to some second-place status in the world. It is kind of like saying, "God wants you to have the best, to prove that he is the best."

The most effective speakers today take a backseat to no one in the secular market in ability to draw convention and arena crowds, as tens of thousands clamor for their presence, their DVDs, their books, and their five-day cruises. Not all achieve the same status, but at whatever their level they have an audience, their message of "having it all," fortified by the assurance that this is the "heart of God" concerning us all, makes them relevant and in quite high demand in Christian media. And all the while they are gaining more and more acceptance in secular media—especially as they sanitize or even omit core Christian themes such as the cross of Christ, judgment, heaven, and hell.

Over thirty years ago as a brand-new believer I cut my teeth on the so-called prosperity gospel, which was a feature of much of the Word of Faith movement in which I was involved. That movement taught that God wants all his children to ooze in material prosperity. I recall that the private airplane was a very important status symbol with many of the prosperity teachers thirty years ago. It was like a validation that one had "arrived" in ministry. They talked in great detail about their private airplanes as I listened intently. They spoke of how God provided for their planes, and how their example was a model for me to expect God to bless me.

I am not aware if there has actually been an internal study to see how many followers of the prosperity gospel actually have airplanes themselves. I am sure there are some. Today, the prosperity message has morphed into an arena-style production of motivational speaking and life-success marketing that makes me long for the good old days. In the good old days, at least some of the prosperity teachers would sometimes get off the singular message of "wealth" and teach valuable principles from the Word of God. And some would at least talk about discipleship before that was replaced by Christian life coaching. Thirty years ago, attaining that private plane seemed to be the gold standard, kind of like the Oscars is for Hollywood. I don't know what the gold standard is today for "Christian" motivational speakers, but I imagine it has changed. Maybe instead of the private plane it is an entire fleet of airplanes!

I am not opposed to airplanes. In fact, I rather prefer them if I have to go from Nashville to San Jose, or from Memphis to Miami. If I owned one and it were legal, I would probably use it to go down the street to Safeway or Kroger to buy milk, or to the airport to get on an even bigger plane. Maybe what I really need is a helicopter, but my children need college.

Pilots for Prosperity Preaching

What does the prosperity gospel in its contemporary package of motivational and success speaking have to do with postmodernism? Everything, when considering the context of a postcard within a postmodern church era. Because, like all postcards, there is a bit of truth in a very narrow focus of what the card says. But as you pull back and look at the entire terrain, what you see in this postmodern installment of prosperity preaching is a validation of the "me" generation, complete with a stark materialism and a philosophy that fosters the personal pursuit of happiness and self-focused temporal desires. It can easily become idolatry because this kind of perspective presupposes that God wants me to realize all my earthly dreams—if I have enough faith. At least it used to be called faith. Now it only requires visualization and "thinking happy thoughts."

Since many in the church subscribe to holistic prosperity as their spiritual right, postmodernism falls into place nicely. It is not just being blessed with money; it is an across-the-board entitlement as a Christian in the postmodern church orthodoxy.

No longer is it sufficient to be in a place of spiritual contentment, as the Bible says, but the prevailing belief now is that all areas of life must reach the place of "the good life" and happiness fulfilled.

The "pilots for prosperity preaching," or P³ as we will call them, have been around for many years. In the interest of full disclosure, I still occasionally listen to the teaching of one who would be considered a P³ icon. He has ministered for thirty-five to forty years, and I listen to him because he has wisdom and insight into the Word. He "flies his plane," so to speak, in air space that is not singularly focused upon prosperity teaching. Then why am I even writing this chapter? The answer is, because I believe the prosperity message, as a one-trick pony, is a symptom of a postmodern church that has its gospel priorities out of whack, and needs to land the plane on the proclamation of knowing Jesus Christ and him crucified.

As a believer who has been a part of the charismatic stream, it galls some that I have listened to John F. MacArthur for over twenty-five years. MacArthur is very opposed to almost all aspects of the charismatic movement, but I listen to him because I believe he is an excellent teacher of the Word. I do not have to agree with him on every single issue to derive great benefit from my overall exposure to someone who is a solid teacher. And by the way, MacArthur has incredible teaching on biblical giving. In the context of the Word of Faith movement, which I was a part of for about three years, I am glad for many of the things I learned about the power of faith in the early days after my conversion, as well as the importance of meditation, confession of the Word, and the inheritance of the believer. Here again, I never bought wholesale into everything that was coming out of WOF teaching, and by 1983–84 I was pretty much out of the movement.

In the context of specific prosperity doctrine, I sensed that the emphasis was nearly always about me, and this was true even if the teachings were couched in terms of "no lack" and "walking in divine health" as a testimony to the power of faith in God and his Word. In other words, it felt like I had more at stake than just my fulfillment of what I was naming to claim. There was also the underlying implication that unless I made sure God made it happen, I would run the risk of having a witness that would not be a winning faith that could draw others to Jesus (even though during those first couple of years after my conversion I know of only one person for sure whom I led to Christ, and the transaction had nothing to do with prosperity teaching).

I began weaning away from the P³ doctrine as I got involved with churches whose emphasis and ministry had little or no association with the prosperity camp, and as I began broadening the scope of both studying and understanding the Scriptures.

Within the P³ culture to which I was exposed, the focus used to be primarily on three themes—health, wealth, and how the activation of my faith is the key to unlocking the health and wealth that God had provided to me by what Jesus did on the cross. And when I would go hear the teachers and preachers, they would often talk about their trips to other countries and "taking the gospel" there. I would sometimes wonder what taking the gospel there actually looked like. What was presented there as the gospel? Was it the need for a Savior for redemption and eternal life, or was it a prosperity gospel tailored for the country and culture they were in? And how did that actually work in a dirt-poor country?

From Naming and Claiming to Begging and Bawling

Certainly God does choose to make some people wealthy, but most Christians are not, except in America when compared to Christians in, say, China or Ukraine. Jesus talked about wealth quite a bit, so I suppose we should not be surprised that God is the ultimate arbiter of wealth. The Lord did not emphasize the wide appeal of being rich so much as issue warnings about its trappings and how it can dominate one's motivation and affection.

Some followers of the prosperity gospel do become very financially blessed in the P³ gospel, and so do other Christians who do not embrace the prosperity message at all. This is because many principles of Scripture are consistent with God's economy, which runs in stark contrast to the world's economy. It is counterintuitive to the natural mind to rest in the assurance that God will take care of one's needs when called or moved to give. That kind of mindset helps release the power that money would otherwise have over us. And it shows just how different the fruit of the Spirit looks from the fruit of the flesh. Those principles of giving also carry the promise that the Lord will be our sufficiency in all we need.

It is the same for the reality of healing. I know that God heals today and that he does so in the realm of the miraculous. I know this because he has done so in dramatic fashion with many people I personally have seen and with my daughter in early 1992. The intense emergency of the moment with my daughter at four years old soon found me claiming and confessing God's healing while melting upon the hospital emergency room floor, begging God and crying out in agony over my daughter. I went from naming and claiming to begging and bawling. But I saw God's healing.

She had been violently stricken with bacterial meningitis after being sick over a weekend. She was unable to speak and in grave danger. And in a miracle she was brought back from the throes of near death and almost certain brain damage that would have led to learning disabilities, possible loss of vision, and hearing impairment, to being completely made whole! It did not happen because my confession was a poster spot for "How to Confess Your Healing."

I do believe this much: Looking retrospectively, I can see that there were many things in play during that entire ordeal. The prayers of the saints from our church and the Christian community as a whole served to raise my wife and me up, if not my daughter, as that first awful day proceeded. We could sense that prayer support in a tangible way.

Perhaps it was their faith and their prayers that invaded heaven, but the testimony to God's goodness and power to heal became a source of great celebration for our family and dear friends at our church when my daughter opened her eyes the second day and looked at me and said, "Daddy, I want a Happy Meal." Her healing was a great testimony of God's goodness to the hospital staff, whose work in the initial critical period of diagnosis was a major factor in stabilizing my daughter. The ER physician who treated her told me a couple of days later that it was one of the worst cases of bacterial meningitis he had ever seen.

Even though it was the darkest twenty-four hours in my life, I know God had not forsaken us. As much as I was at first reduced to a puddle on the floor, Camille and I never even considered that the Lord was not with us every step of the way. His love for our family was beyond doubt.

We are keenly aware that God both sovereignly and miraculously saved her, not only from grave danger but to a complete absence of any residual problems from the disease—not one! This even included my daughter's having no memory of any pain or discomfort. It was like it never happened. But it did happen, and we have this great testimony to the goodness of God.

We will forever give thanks to God for his kindness and mercy. He is the God who heals, by whatever means he chooses. I just do not make demands upon him or his Word in the absence of not embracing the knowledge of his love for me. And in that we trust.

This incident with my daughter also served to remind us that God had many things happening around this crisis. We also witnessed this amazing mobilization of God's people to pray fervently and without ceasing. It was both an organized corporate effort and individuals who went to the mat on behalf of our daughter. The outpouring of care from the body of Christ to my family was beyond what we could have imagined. It was a divinely coordinated case of God sending people to us at different times to say just the right thing to help us keep perspective.

Maybe her affliction had something to do with the Lord wanting the body of Christ and the local church to see the fruit of a call to action and prayer response by the saints of God. Perhaps someone else's faith quotient was energized by the ordeal. Maybe it was all of the above.

That is the thing about the sovereignty of God. It has all these purposes going off at the same time, like the beauty of a fireworks finale at a Fourth of July celebration. Everything is bursting forth, exploding in sound and color, lighting up the night sky, even orchestrated to music. Yet many times, as it is with God, one does not see the divine orchestration until the fifth of July.

So it is with the providence of God. Who can know the divine ways? Yet we know he loves us and that "in all things God works for the good of those who love him, who have been called according to his purpose" (Rom. 8:28 NIV).

Providence: More than the Capital of Rhode Island

My own journey and subsequent twenty-five-year observation of the P^3 doctrine informs my view that there is a problem with the application of faith. I do realize that without faith it is impossible to please God, and yet in the P^3 economy (health, wealth, and the activation of my faith), faith itself almost becomes the object of my faith, instead of Jesus being the object of my faith.

By emphasis, faith *in faith* sort of becomes the coequal to *faith in Christ*. It is not what is overtly advocated, but once again it is the unintended consequence. It has the effect of *faith* becoming almost a fourth member of the Trinity, instead of the measure we are given by which we are able to come to, and please, God. I am certainly not advocating less faith, and I readily acknowledge my need for more faith in my walk. But the *singular application of faith* related to the *preoccupation with earthly wealth* within the prosperity creed takes far too much of the attention of many believers. It has the effect of keeping the Christian focused more upon temporal things than having their life available to the transformational and conforming work of the Holy Spirit. The work of sanctification is not immediate, and it may not always feel like a week at Sandals Resort in the Bahamas. The instant gratification of earthly wealth can easily be more attractive.

A bedrock P^3 and motivational speaker belief is that the Devil is the author of all sickness and poverty, along with generally any inconvenience we might be forced to endure. In this teaching, it is insulting, if not heresy, to assign such responsibility to God.

That certainly reinforces a cultural view of God among those in the church who assert that he would surely not subject his children to any undue outside pressure. Now I know within the context of writing the story about my daughter that it was the Devil who tried to kill her, destroy her, and steal from us. Yet I also know that this whole incident did not escape God's awareness, and that he had control over the whole encounter. At least in a macro sense, it would be accurate to say, "God allowed it to happen." Both realities were present at the same time, even though ultimately it would be God's will that would prevail.

How can it be any other way? He is omniscient, so that in knowing everything he certainly knew about the attack of bacterial meningitis. He knew about it in every detail. It could not have been a sneak attack. He is also omnipotent, meaning all-powerful, so he certainly had the power to prevent it, just as he had the power to prevent all the troubling attacks against Job in the Old Testament.

When we are in difficult circumstances, we cannot compartmentalize God by ignoring who he is and declaring he has no hand, at least in a broad sense, in anything bad that happens. Somehow we have to get hold of the notion that God allows things to happen, without assigning a negative motive to him. He can do it because he is God.

And that leads to the next P^3 dilemma, which is the problem of some people taking Scripture out of context. When I was in graduate school, I took a class on hermeneutics, which is a fancy word for approaching the interpretation of Scripture. One of the ways to accurately interpret the Bible is to determine what the author intended to say (which is not quite the same as assigning a meaning to a verse based upon what I intend for it to say). In applying this principle, I learned, for example, that the parable of the sower has nothing to do with finances but everything to do with receiving the gospel. Context is important to reach accurate conclusions, because one has to look at the whole body of Scripture on any given topic in order to find all the threads of that topic in the Bible.

Many preachers and teachers flip the whole thing around and start with their conclusion, and then find all kinds of Scripture to take out of context to prove that their conclusion is correct. In so doing, the context of Scripture may experience a sudden loss of cabin pressure.

The proposition that all things bad are always directly authored by the Devil presents some doctrinal problems, unless you throw Job out of the plane at thirty thousand feet. This dovetails nicely into the next P^3 problem, which is the whole issue of the sovereignty of God, for which you will not find many tape offers, either out in the lobby of the coliseum, or in the seat-back pockets of the ten-seater plane.

Many Christians seem to believe the providence of God is little more than the capital of Rhode Island. Which, by the way, those of you on the left side of the cabin are able to see as we fly over. Be sure to wave, because this plane hardly ever lands there.

The prosperity gospel teaches that the claimed verses of Scripture become rock-solid laws that are etched in stone. And who can argue that on its face?

God does not violate his Word—even if some prosperity-gospel adherents choose to take it completely out of context. He is the integrity of his Word. The prosperity gospel asserts that our faith can make demands upon that Word because we are believing what God has said right there in black and white. And with Jesus' death, burial, and resurrection, it is ours to claim because he has won it for us—praise God! Furthermore, believers in the prosperity gospel make verses like Philippians 4:19 do double duty: "And my God will meet all your needs according to his glorious riches in Christ Jesus" (NIV).

Yet here the P^3 creed hits turbulence, because now we activate our faith to believe that in place of the word "needs" we may freely substitute and insert … anything. God will provide a large sum of money, an airplane, a brand-new car, a fat bank account, a job promotion, the winning lotto ticket, new hair growth, or whiter teeth, all according to his glorious riches in Christ Jesus. I think we may have just hit an air pocket.

Different Kinds of Giving in God's Economy

God's principles of finances are Word-tested and true. We do open access to the blessing of God as we give generously to churches, the poor, missions, and people in need. We love to give testimony in our family when God provides finances and favor, and we have taught our children to glorify him when they see the principles of God in play and to recognize that he is taking care of their needs and blessing them. But it is just not a dollar-for-dollar transaction in God's economy. He is not a branch of the heavenly ATM. Neither does it necessarily mean we are not in faith if we are experiencing pressures in our finances. It is all about trusting God, regardless of the circumstances.

The Bible speaks about different kinds of giving in God's economy. There is *purposed* giving, which is directive, regular, and practiced with a disposition of joy and cheerfulness. And there is *spontaneous* giving, which addresses specific individual and corporate ministry needs that may arise. Both are directed by the Holy Spirit and both are acts of faith. Inherent in any biblical giving is the element of praise and sacrifice—or sacrificial giving. Here, the more the believer is able to embrace, the more the reality of God's goodness is realized. It is a wonderful way to live, but it is not a one-to-one equivalence. It is not a mathematical equation because these are principles, not laws. And the principles are not just bound to finances. God's economy is much broader than just riches.

If these principles were laws, there would not be so many qualifiers in the Bible. For example, in the book of James we are told we do not receive what we ask from the Lord because *our motives are not right.* So the law is, in fact, qualified by the motivations of our heart. That constitutes a condition that is more than just determined by faith.

Jesus said, "Seek first the kingdom of God, and all these things shall be added to you"(Matt. 6:33). We may presume from that statement that if I am not seeking God and his kingdom first and foremost, then I may have a problem receiving temporal things. The principle being that if we have set our hearts and minds on temporal things, we are divided in our attention and affection to God.

Then there is the whole principle of having our faith tested by having temporal things taken away. If Job has parachuted safely in Providence from his ejection out of the plane, you can ask him. Or just read his book again.

Jesus also said I run the possibility of choking on my preoccupation with riches, and that this may indicate I have a much bigger problem—misplaced motivations at least, and evidence of a false conversion at worst. And make no mistake, much of the P^3 gospel by definition has you preoccupied, almost like an accountant with a ledger and a tally sheet.

The Lord also said that we would have "trouble" in this life, and that this trouble was a mark of being his disciple. When our finances come under pressure, we pray against any demonic design that is at work. Then we affirm God's control over whatever is happening. No matter what occurs in this particular incident, we know we are loved by him, and that his glory and our ultimate good will assure the outcome.

One of the favorite lines of the prosperity pilot is "God's word on finances and healing is like the law of gravity, only it's more sure than gravity." If I had a dollar for every time I heard that from 1979 until 1982, I would be lending money to Bill Gates.

The sovereignty of God is this wonderful attribute about who the Lord is and how he chooses to weave and orchestrate everything for his purposes and our good. Gravity is a natural law that works 99.99 percent of the time.

Except when God has other plans.

He flipped gravity, and probably every law of hydraulics, upside down when he parted the Red Sea. His sovereignty makes marvelous exceptions to natural laws. Suddenly, water defied the law of gravity and proceeded in its uncontained form upward from the seabed and must have even been pulled from side to side, creating a suspended sea wall up in the air on both sides—out of itself—and did so for a period of time that allowed passage of probably a couple million people. And God did it again when Joshua led the tribes across the Jordan ...

during flood season. As the priests touched the water nineteen miles upstream, the water heaped up and stood on itself so that the nation of Israel could cross. Thank God we had the law of gravity to make that happen. As they say, "What goes up, must come down"—unless God says it stays up.

God will stand natural law on its head to accomplish his purposes, just as in the case of stopping the earth's rotation with Joshua, or causing otherwise dumb scavenging birds to bring carry-out dinner to a depressed prophet named Elijah. That is the thing about the providence of God. It is working all the time to produce his will. If we could see all the mechanisms in natural law or the weaving of circumstances that go into making "coincidences," we would all be brought to our knees at the intricacy and precision of how God does what he does.

All God has to do is defy natural law one time, and that law's certainty is revealed to be subservient to God's sovereignty. If a donkey can talk, or if a bush can be totally engulfed in flames without the fire consuming one leaf, we might want to consider reclassifying the law to a principle.

I am not sure when the saying "as sure as the sun comes up tomorrow" came on the scene, but I imagine it was not within a thousand years from when Joshua and his people saw that that did *not happen*. God's Word is true. He is the integrity of his Word. It is performed according to his will, which sometimes even supersedes our own. Imagine that.

P³ preachers, motivational speakers, and itchy-eared congregants need to land the plane and proclaim the true gospel that saves men's souls. Everything else will be added according to God's will within the context of our pursuit of him and his purposes for us. He is good!

Mr. and Mrs. Decision-maker, Come on Down!

REMEMBER *THE PRICE is Right*—the show where someone in a bad T-shirt would be called out when his or her name was drawn to be a contestant? They would be convulsing and contorting with ecstatic glee as they ran down front to greet Bob Barker (or, more lately, Drew Carey), whose hair color changed more frequently than Dennis Rodman's. They didn't have to win anything. It was just the invitation to "come on down" that was the thrill.

By contrast, don't you just love getting invitations to places or events you would really rather not attend? You know, the ones like the wedding invitation from your wife's third cousin whom you met only once, but because you met at *your* wedding you are now compelled to be included among the *dearly beloved* who get together in Buffalo, New York, the last Saturday in January (and you haven't even paid for Christmas yet). That kind of invitation?

Even our aforementioned trip to the Big Island, which was otherwise great, found us at midweek with an invitation slipped under our hotel suite inviting us to a luau. It was our acceptance of that invitation that forever made me vow *never* to read past, "You are cordially invited to attend …" whatever it is!

Camille and I, along with our son, stood in a line for one and a half hours—a line that wrapped around the entire grounds to the entrance of the luau. Only, the grounds were not actually "grounds." They were concrete pavers. So we stood there with the angle of the late afternoon sun bearing down upon us, with no bathroom, no water, and me wearing a black shirt, in the middle of July. Had I not moved around and changed positions constantly, I would have certainly been poached within a matter of seconds. The line was long, with the average age of people in the line being probably near seventy-five.

You see, this was the "early bird" luau, so when we finally got herded in, I instantly became "Sonny" to everyone at my table. The people were great and very friendly, and we tried adding to the conversation as much as possible. But we just were not up to speed with the lexicon of geriatric medicines, and they were the topic *du jour*. We just smiled a lot and kept saying how much we hoped "that clears up real soon."

The food was an entirely different matter, as it too had been lined up for at least one and a half hours prior to our one and a half hours before entering the feast. Approaching the salad was dangerous, and I will never again use the term "wilted" to describe lettuce that has only begun to dry up and fray a little at the edges. Because at our luau, un-fresh, sun-exposed, un-chilled, unrecognizable lettuce was called "just a bit impaired, not wilted." It was like saying, "Armageddon might get a little rough."

Also, I kept looking for the roasted pig like in the movies. Or how about just a hamburger at this sixty-bucks-per-plate blowout? But no, I got eel stuffed in another big ugly fish's mouth, whose eyes were staring at me (which I am told are suitable for eating as well). And our island vegetables looked a whole lot like the pine cones and exotic monkey grass that were part of the landscape outside our suite. In fact, all the fish were big and ugly, and they all retained their eyes. It is possible there was a jailbreak at an exotic fish aquarium and all the fish escaped to this luau.

The floor show was good, but we were starving from not eating anything at the all-you-can-eat fish-eye buffet. The show ended at 7:30 PM with one of the performers eating fire while jumping on a table to do a war dance. That produced the only casualty of the night, when one older gentleman received medical attention after he passed out—as it was his table the fire-eater chose to jump upon while belching out a war hoop that would scare every demon on the island.

We said our good-byes very quickly and rushed out of the area to return to our hotel, where we debriefed about our luau experience, ate macadamia nuts, and convinced ourselves that we really did not go, that we had all just taken a nap and dreamed it.

Hence, I am probably a little jaded when it comes to invitations in general. I get this feeling I might end up at a fish-eye luau in Buffalo at the end of January. And I am very jaded when it comes to invitations as decisions for salvation in the postmodern church. They are called "decisions," but many times they bear little resemblance to what Scripture prescribes for salvation because they mostly fail at telling the decision-makers most of what they need to know. The decision invitation is the quintessential *methodology trumping the message* in the postmodern church.

"Soul Winning" in America's Postmodern Churches

Methodology often trumps message in our individual witnessing. We presume that leading someone in a "sinner's prayer" is tantamount to winning a soul for the kingdom of Christ. Yet that may or may not be the case. It is all about what is shared, what we say to provoke people into really thinking about their lives in light of what the gospel says. It is not about getting them up the aisle and to the altar to make a decision based upon incomplete and many times inaccurate information.

Besides, the very premise of our deciding about our salvation is itself questionable. Is salvation something that I decide, or that I decide with God, or does he decide it all because I am "spiritually dead?" Clearly, God is the initiator, and it is his grace that opens our hearts. But that's another book, I suppose.

I do not wish to communicate a formula that takes its place among the modern methods of evangelism, but clearly there are important things that need to be communicated to people, whether we are sharing one-on-one or speaking to a crowd. In presenting the gospel, we must tell the person with whom we are sharing who God is. If we do not give them the God of the Bible, as Paul Washer says, "They will create one in their own image." His attributes must be shared so that people who hear the gospel message clearly know to whom they are indebted. Then there is disclosure of the violation of God's righteous and holy morality, the introduction of the law, which is designed to confront and crush any vestige of self-righteousness (as is one of its designations), and the fact of our helpless inability to pay a debt that will render a clear judgment. Then we go from the law to grace by telling them about Jesus—his atonement (the only sufficient sacrifice to satisfy the wrath of God so that we stay out of hell, which is what we deserve for our crimes), the cross, and the resurrection. They must repent, be sorry and forsake their sin, and put their faith in Jesus for eternal salvation. And if we really do care about where they go from here, we must tell them the truth that disciples of Jesus will have trouble in this life, and following Jesus will be costly. But, they will be given peace by the Holy Spirit, who will cover them, guide them, and empower them to live to glorify God, while preserving those who are his until the end.

And since Jesus spoke of it often, we would be incomplete in our witnessing if we did not emphasize that a follower of Christ will bear fruit that will evidence the marks of true conversion and discipleship. Indeed, it is a growth process, a perfecting that will never be perfect while living this life. And there will be ongoing struggles with the flesh that will inevitably bring times where we will certainly sin. However, true Christians will humbly walk before God and clothe themselves in the advocacy and Lordship of Jesus Christ through the grace of the Holy Spirit. And their lives will evidence that Lordship.

Unfortunately for soul winning in today's postmodern church, the doctrines of this age are ever present many times in the way salvation gets preached, as well as in how we have come to witness to people. We tend to focus on the felt-needs emphasis, which can often trump the true need for salvation, because the true need may not get disclosed. In the postmodern mindset, there is an incomplete view of God, human-centeredness instead of God-centeredness, the focus on "my decision" without regard for the work of the Holy Spirit; the near, if not complete, absence of authentic repentance, the "good life" hook, and the sinner's prayer, which allows someone besides God to declare my salvation.

At its core, the postmodern witnessing methodology has been developed to make the salvation transaction simple and easy. When Jesus said that one must come to him "as a child," he was not referring to the "ease" with which salvation is secured. Rather, he was referring to *humility*, the state of coming to Christ in childlike trust while overcoming all remnants of an arrogance and self-righteousness that suggest we have anything to do with being saved. Both the grace to be drawn to the Lord and the faith to trust in him come from God. They are his gifts to us, wrought by the grace of the Holy Spirit.

That grace to make Jesus *Savior* is compounded by the work of the Spirit in the life of the believer to make Jesus *Lord* of the one who is saved. If you wanted to read all the passages where Jesus talked about the ease of walking daily as his disciple, you would have a surprisingly short read. As a matter of fact, the Gospel of John shows that the more Jesus revealed himself as the "I am," the less the people could handle it, and the more the crowds scattered. Even those who had been beneficiaries of his healing miracles, as well as having had their bellies filled by his supernatural provision of food, could not get past the offense of Jesus' claims about himself. You combine those themes with what Jesus says in all the Gospels about self-denial, persecution, taking up crosses daily, and being hated by the world, and it's clearly only by grace through faith that we are going to be able to endure till the end.

Yet this is not about determining salvation based upon degree of difficulty, suggesting that somehow making the gospel harder to grasp makes it more authentic. The biblical notion of salvation is about *degree of truth* in what is being proclaimed in the gospel invitation in light of a supernatural encounter by the Holy Spirit.

The Street Version

"God loves you and has a fantastic plan for your life!" (Incidentally, that plan would include persecution, trouble, pressures, and a command to deny yourself. And by the way, who is this God who loves you?)

"See, we've all sinned. That's what separates us from God, and that's what keeps us from being happy. We have to ask God to forgive us." (By the way, what is sin?)

"If you just ask Jesus to come into your heart, he will forgive your sins and you can go to heaven. That's all you have to do." (Who is Jesus, and how does he come into my heart? And why would I want to go to heaven, whatever heaven is?)

"It really is easy. All you have to do is say this prayer with me and believe. I am going to lead you in that prayer. You just repeat it after me—unless it makes you uncomfortable, then I will just say the prayer out loud. It will only take a couple of minutes; that's all!" (Remind me again, how many times is this prayer model even suggested in Scripture? What passage recounts Jesus or anyone else practicing this method?)

"In just a moment when we pray, you're going to be saved. Then you can live your life in the way that God will lead you, and he will always be with you. Now, you have to mean it. The only requirement is that you are sincere. That's what faith is. Times might get tough, but God will make things work out for you. Now you can know what true happiness is, and then you will be with him for all eternity in heaven." (Thank God that the one who is sharing is willing to do all the work in this salvation transaction. If this is really who God is, it's not a bad deal at all.)

Then the witnessing concludes with this Christian's version of the sinner's prayer, along with the attending declarations that the witnessee has been saved and set free. And maybe he has.

The Pulpit Version

Far too often, the soul-winning script hardly varies from the street version to the pulpit version. And even if the message is slightly more biblically based in the pulpit version, the outcome remains the same—the message of salvation is many times compromised by the ease of the altar call decision. The altar call invitation as a method is about 175 years old. It was *not* practiced by the great preachers who helped shape America's spiritual fortunes, such as John Wesley, Jonathan Edwards, and George Whitefield, all great preachers and theologians who spread the gospel while seeing thousands come to salvation in America during the eighteenth century.

The practice of the altar call was mainstreamed by Charles Finney who, from the mid 1830's, used the invitation as a way to "get people involved" in the public ownership of their salvation. Many works have been written on how effective Finney's revivals actually were. The reviews by many theological historians indicate his use of the altar call was less than always effective as evidenced by follow-up studies.

No doubt God has brought many people to salvation as they responded in faith and went forward to the altar. It is a heart thing, and if one's heart has been pricked by the grace of the Holy Spirit, that person will experience redemption. But an invitation without properly explaining how salvation is gained will sometimes turn into a form of *decisionism* that is reinforced by another person declaring the salvation of someone as sealed and complete. How does this happen? It occurs as drama is created in an appeal to "come down to the altar"—or stay at their seat and "do something" as just the right music is being played to enhance the emotions.

This kind of drama is usually without the complete message of the gospel that is able to confront the will with law and grace. And it omits the knowledge from the whole counsel of the Word to bring the will to contrition and repentance, and, therefore, change. Accordingly, the will, and ultimately the mind itself, is not changed because the law (knowledge of sin) and our transgression of it has not been fully disclosed. What is left far too often is the emotional experience that begins to fade as the days go by.

Should the emotions be affected by the gospel? Of course. There is no way they could not be. Every part of our being would be engaged in the act of responding to the Holy Spirit. The point is that if the will is not confronted and crushed by the law of the gospel, then it could be that only the emotions are activated. If that happens, the will may not be changed at all. Thus, two years down the road, the person who made the decision may show very little, if any, evidence of a changed life. And it is often the case that he or she becomes inoculated from the true gospel, believing he or she is saved because of the prior emotional decision and its validation by some well-meaning authority figure.

God saves those whom he will through this method of soul winning—but in spite of it, not because of it. I do not doubt some of my readers came to Christ by this method, as God is certainly able to open the heart of the sinner. I do not dispute that one can be saved through this method, or any other method, but I am saying the method itself does not save anybody. It is the true message of the gospel that opens the heart, as was the case with Lydia in Acts 16.

Public Decisionism

Public decisionism has the effect of compelling people to overcome their embarrassment and humiliation, leave their comfortable seats, and publically confess Christ to agree with the apostle Paul that "I am not ashamed of the gospel, because it is the power of God for the salvation of everyone who believes" (Rom. 1:16 NIV).

That is, in fact, very true. Still, if we still neglect to tell people what salvation actually is—to reveal the whole counsel of God—then the act of walking down an aisle and being victorious over public embarrassment can be confused for salvation. What usually follows this public display is a pastor or some other Christian leader at the altar leading the penitent in the sinner's prayer, or the filling out of a commitment card, after which they are hereby and forever more declared—*saved!*

The real saving transaction shows that a person recognizes their sin and their need for a relationship with God through Jesus. Only time and the spiritual fruit produced by a person's life will tell if public decisionism actually leads to that kind of a relationship.

Some even use the *portable remote model* for decision invitations as well—the kind that are done without having anyone leave the comfort his or her seat. It is designed usually for when it is time for the service to be over but you still want people to get saved before they get to the Olive Garden in anticipation of beating the noon church crowd.

Does this example of the remote model sound familiar?

With every head bowed, and every eye closed, in a moment I'm going to pray. If you are sincere, by faith, you can ask Jesus into your heart, and he will come. The Bible says that if we confess with our mouth and believe in our hearts, we will be saved. That's all you have to do. I know it's getting late, but this will only take a moment. You can make the most important decision of your life today! So I want everyone to pray out loud with me. Let's say this together. "Lord Jesus, I confess that I am a sinner. I believe you died for my sins and rose again and defeated death. I believe you, and I believe you have saved me right now. I confess with my mouth that you rose from the dead and are Lord and Savior, and that I have eternal life in you.

In Jesus' name, amen.

Well, you all have a great week, and we'll see you on Wednesday night!

Again, this method would be less questionable if the focus were more on a complete message of salvation before the method was initiated.

Another method used in public decisionism (which is actually less than public) is the *raise your hand if you helped me win the Oscar* version of the *portable remote model* of salvation invitation. It is quite the opposite from the invitation that is more public, like walking down an aisle or praying the sinner's prayer. This procedure relies upon *stealth* as a means of preventing any personal embarrassment.

If you don't know Jesus, I'm just going to ask you, with every head bowed and every eye closed, to gently slip up your hand. Go ahead, just raise your hand. I believe that there are some here today who want to make that decision. If you believe and want to be saved, just go ahead and raise your hand. I'll just take one more moment here. I see that hand, sir; thank you. Thank you, ma'am, in the back, yes, I see you. Thank you. Yes, thank you. Is there one more? I believe there is one more. Yes, over here to my right; I see your hand, madam. Thank you, thank you, thank you!

The gratitude for raising hands is so profound that sometimes the minister starts sounding like he or she is giving an acceptance speech for having won the Oscar for Best Supporting Role for Decisionism in Ending a Sunday Service.

Do we wave at everyone as they run to the altar and fill out a card? Or, do we initiate the CIA special-ops covert method that assures our identity is known only to God, unless someone peeked during the prayer? Whatever decisionism style of invitation that is employed, when the decisions for salvation are made, there seems to be almost an institutional lack of acknowledgment, celebration, and fanfare. No matter what happens at the altar or in the pew, we still get "Amen. See you next week. Hope the Cowboys win today!"

You would think that if heaven is rejoicing at the conversion of even one new believer we might at least have some public acknowledgment, some congregational ownership into the life of the decision-maker. We do it when we christen babies. We have everybody in the congregation stand and repeat some vow that acknowledges our congregational desire to "cover" the child—which I agree with wholeheartedly. And almost everybody is involved. There are the parents, the grandparents, the fifth cousins, the neighbors, their insurance agent, the baby's godparents, and the baby's future third grade teacher. Everybody is there to witness the event and to be a part of the moment. And rightfully so. Why this is not done for decisions to receive Christ is beyond me.

Salvation has become passé, I suppose.

Or perhaps the scripts are so worn and the methods so ineffective that decisions many times have taken the place of true conversions. Salvations get reduced to some end-of-the year statistical report, if emphasized at all.

On the other hand, there is something very dynamic about many of the people Jesus ministered to and whose sins he forgave. They start popping up everywhere and following him into all kinds of places they were not supposed to be, breaking cultural and social codes of the day, just to be around him. They were chastised by the Pharisees and many times ostracized by their own families, but they just kept coming around.

They were changed. People in the congregations, as well as the hometowns, noticed. When someone is born again, it should be a noticeable, corporately emphasized, big deal.

The reason decisionism and its methods are deficient is because we have not given the convert enough accurate information to make an informed decision. Way too often the information they get is shallow and incomplete. Generally speaking, they are given an incomplete picture of who God is and how the sinner has violated God's standard of perfect holiness by breaking his commandments.

If we *do* tell them they need to repent, we seldom tell them what real repentance looks like, other than "changing your mind." We say very little about the cost of following Christ, or that a person who is truly born again will abide in Jesus and produce ongoing spiritual fruit. We tell them that all they have to do is confess with their mouth and believe in their heart, as if that is a one-time event, rather than what C. H. Spurgeon calls "the working out of that which God has worked in."

One can claim the validity of that one-time confession, but if going forward there remains little or no fruit or evidence of conversion, that may indicate there is a severe problem—no matter how many times one says one prayed a prayer with someone based upon Romans 10:9–10 (confessing with the mouth and believing in the heart) and then made a subsequent decision for Christ.

Decisionism as a means of salvation is highly overrated. But it remains the evangelism of choice for most churches in the postmodern age.

What Fruits Are Produced?

It is very enlightening to consider how the different streams of the church apply the tenets of preaching the gospel as related to witnessing methods and the use of public invitations for salvation. Growing up in the United Methodist Church, I do not recall an emphasis upon the salvation invitation. My family was very active. We never missed church unless there was a sickness at home or a movie star in town. We were blessed in that the former rarely happened on a Sunday, and the latter never happened at all.

At twelve years old, as was the custom, I took confirmation classes to "join my faith with the church." In the whole of that transaction I remember hearing about John Wesley, our founder, and that I received a nice Revised Standard Version Bible with my name engraved on the cover. I do not recall if my salvation was discussed or what methods were employed to confirm my status. I am not saying my salvation was not discussed; I just do not have any memory of it. I did stay in the church until I was nineteen, yet at best, I was what Wesley called "almost Christian." I remained mired in the arrogance and hubris of sin until God's grace drew me to Christ and I was saved at age twenty-three in late 1979.

I continue to read Wesley's sermons and his teachings, and I often wonder what it would be like if he were around today and what impact his preaching would have on today's Methodist church.

As I mentioned before, my church life as a Christian for over thirty years has been primarily of the charismatic stream, such as involvement in the Vineyard Association churches. I have also been involved in churches that were a kind of hybrid between charismatic and former denominational bodies.

I cannot speak for the entirety of the charismatic or Pentecostal traditions, for I know there are denominations (such as Assemblies of God and Church of God) that are more salvation-message oriented. But for the most part, in the non-denominational and independent churches there has not been a strategic emphasis upon getting people saved, primarily because the logical assumption would be that you would not be seeking the "deeper things" of the Spirit if you did not already belong to Christ. In fact, you would be quite miserable.

This does not represent any church's official position; it is just the one I have attributed to our movement as a result of thirty years of observation. There is a lot of "retro speak" about salvation, where people talk about getting saved way back "in the denomination" or "when the Lord saved me," as if it were almost a relic of our heritage. Yet the observation is also one for which I am both very deeply concerned and very perplexed. How does anyone move forward spiritually without acknowledging what I believe to be the eight-hundred-pound gorilla in the room? Many of our churches are operating under the assumption that their people have long-since received salvation and have been filled with the Spirit, when clearly both parts of that assumption are in some need of review.

Why do I make such an assertion?

I make the assertion because of the fruit of what many churches in the charismatic renewal are producing. There is such a near epidemic of calling anything or anyone that comes on the horizon a "move of God" that we quickly embrace and too quickly endorse without any historical or biblical consideration or framework. There is way too much preoccupation with the subjective experiential encounter—so much so that many times the encounter gets elevated to a coequal status with God's Word. I know that of which I speak, for I have done it.

In many cases, the culture of the "charismatic conference" has created an *event focus mentality.* I am off to another conference because I need to go get yet another "word from God," or more conference buzz about anything called "prophetic," or the latest news on "third heaven" visitations. I am talking about degree here. I have helped to host and work at conferences, and I have attended them for years. Many of them have been a great help. But as a personal decision, I attend very few, if any, conferences these days. The last conference I attended was a "Grace of Repentance" conference at Jeff Noblitt's church in Muscle Shoals, Alabama. It was near the end of my own six-month repentance season, so it made the conference even more timely and amazing. To say it was not charismatic would be the understatement of the century. I was a closet charismatic for those three days, but that was my own preoccupation. The conference was rich.

What I am suggesting is that the whole conference gaggle can become almost addictive and we can become so event focused that the main and plain disciplines of our Christian faith—Bible study, fasting, prayer, and being encouraged through expository preaching of God's Word—are becoming dulled by comparison to someone's recent revelatory nugget.

Yet more and more, as is the case in the postmodern church, we are getting less exposure in the knowledge of the important historical doctrines of the church, and more with subjective "spiritual discoveries," as well as other postmodern creeds of "me first" in everything. If you don't believe the "me first" preoccupations, then I have two words for you: *church hopping.* And all the charismatic pastors said … "Amen!" On the other hand, maybe a *shout out* is in order to some of the "hoppers" for leaving some of these places that probably need to be left, if not changed in emphasis and practice. And many of the transient parishioners said, "Amen!"

In the tradition of all moves of God, including all the great revivals and renewal visitations that have legitimately been graces from the throne of heaven, it is my prayer that we experience a deep and abiding move of repentance in our churches. I remain convinced that it is a grace that is desperately needed—in wholesale manner.

I hope we can be counted among those who are so fervent for the gospel that we embrace the resolve of Paul, who said, "For I determined not to know anything among you except Jesus Christ and Him crucified" (1 Cor. 2:2).

That verse would be a great title and theme for a conference.

In the meantime, why not issue an invitation across every stream of Christianity? Let us invite one another to do away with decision evangelism entirely. At least until we give the ones who are deciding the information they decidedly need to really decide about their decision. And while we are at it, we may want to ask what God may be deciding about us?

The Full-color Travel Brochure

You never outgrow the meaning of the Gospel—
We are strengthened by the Gospel by God till we die—
You never outgrow the need to preach to yourself the Gospel.
—John Piper

Who Is God?

IN JUST A glimpse, the incomplete answer to this question is he is the eternal, one God, who is outside time and space. He is self-sufficient. He is self-existent, with no beginning and no end. Neither is he bound by any metric that any convention would seek to impose. God is the Creator whose majesty and splendor is unsurpassed. Creation displays his majesty and the heavens declare his glory.

God is good and merciful beyond what words of goodness and mercy could describe. He is full of lovingkindness and he is longsuffering and unfathomably patient with the sinner. He is the all complete and eternally powerful, all-knowing and all-present God. There is nothing that is not known by him …

nothing. God is just. His scales are balanced to the perfection of justice and the perfection of his goodness. He is faithful and he is sovereign. He is complete in his righteousness. He is love. He is an awesome, consuming fire.

God is holy.

The holiness of God is one of the most prevailing realities in Scripture concerning his transactions with human beings from the earliest point. God came to Abraham in a vision, saying, "Do not be afraid, Abram. I am your shield, your exceedingly great reward" (Gen. 15:1). God would often "speak" to Abraham through his own voice, which normally had the effect of taking the patriarch to his knees. If God did not speak directly, an angel would often do God's bidding.

Yet by the time Moses arrived on the scene, God was ready to "hear the cries" of his children in the captivity of Egypt and bring about a miraculous deliverance. At the same time, he initiated the means by which he would be among his people.

Now in absolute, consummate living color, the children of Israel are introduced to an entirely new level of the holiness of the Lord. They have been told of his holiness, but now they become the firsthand recipients of its terrible and magnificent power. Even Moses, who was the undisputed mediator between God and the people, could not look upon God directly and live. Why? Because of the unbridgeable contrast between God's holiness and Moses' sinful humanity. Yet the Lord proceeds with what he has decreed. *He is going to be among his people.*

God is holy in the completeness of *pure* moral purity and the absence of any hint or shadow of impurity. It is the immaculacy of his own purity that makes his holiness preeminent and eternally pure. In all of his other attributes, God is intrinsically holy. He is holy in his judgment, faithfulness, sovereignty, love, righteousness, and mercy. Holiness is the essence of who the Father is.

R. C. Sproul gives an amazing insight from the sixth chapter of Isaiah when commenting on the holiness of God:

> The Bible says that God is holy, holy, holy. Not that He is merely holy, or even holy, holy. He is holy, holy, holy. The Bible never says that God is love, love, love, or mercy, mercy, mercy, or wrath, wrath, wrath, or justice, justice, justice. It does say that He is holy, holy, holy, the whole earth is full of His glory.[1]

It stands beyond any doubt that if the angels are going to spend eternity declaring the holiness of God, as the Bible says they will, then they have seen something so incredible in just that one attribute to elicit an eternity of ecstatic response.

We are compelled to recapture the fullness of the truth of God's holiness, because it is only in that context that we understand our history with God and our destiny as heaven's children. As the church embraces, teaches, cries out for, and in all other ways acknowledges the holiness of God, it will make pale the ancillary things that have captured our attention but have yielded little fruit by comparison.

Much of the postmodern church, as evidenced by their church life emphasis, seems to have settled for a very minimal view of pursuing the holiness of God. For many of us, it has been reduced to an occasional mention from the pulpit or in a chorus of a song, but far too often, it is a casual pursuit.

If that sounds judgmental, let me assure you that both my eyes require drops several times a day on account of the attending soreness from my pulling logs out of them. I have not mastered the knowledge of the holiness of God, let alone conquered the art of walking it out. If the lack of such knowledge were analogous to population density in small area, mine would be the combined population of India and China—on Rhode Island! I am a work in progress, to say the least, with a long way to go, to say even less.

Like many in the postmodern church, I have elevated other interests with the result of settling for its casual contact and cameo appearance here and there in the privacy of my room or in the corporate meeting of church.

Many in today's church, as is true regarding doctrinal matters generally, have little knowledge and even less understanding of the holiness of God. It is critical for the church to know that it is the holiness of God we have violated that has, in part, formed our predicament. Yet at the same time, as believers we are told to "be holy," which is something God expects and which, of course, can be done only through the help of the Holy Spirit.

But how does one walk in holiness? How does it actually happen? Because even by the Spirit, it seems like a daunting task. And if we don't stop here and immediately insert the word *grace* after the word *task*, then faster than Lon Chaney Jr. turned into the Wolfman, we'll quickly turn into a Pharisee. And though we may not grow fangs and howl at the moon, we will encounter a worse fate from clinging to a form or dictate of the law of holiness through compulsion instead of compassion, without the means of grace to keep anything but a tired shadow of that law. I recently heard a message by John Piper illustrating this point from the story in John's gospel where Jesus encounters a woman caught in adultery. Piper encourages us that what remains out of that encounter is the ever-present command for our walking in holiness, as Jesus tells the woman, "Go and sin no more." However, she is empowered to do so on account of the Lord's amazing grace he shows by assuring her, "Neither do I condemn you." Out of her experience of Jesus' *grace* to protect her and forgive her, the commandment to be *holy* is no longer an insurmountable obstacle or a stale, Pharisaical pursuit, but rather an act of love for one who has been set free. The same course is set for us, as it's the ongoing experience of grace in our lives to be fully submitted to the Spirit's work of holiness in us, making the yoke easy and the burden light.

There is this amazing revelation about the holiness of God as revealed throughout the book of Leviticus. I have recently read it again and have done so with a fresh awe and amazement of the Lord's love for us by virtue of gaining a new understanding of the breadth of his holiness. It is just a fractional glimpse, but its revelation has been very eye opening. This has not always been the case when it came time for reading this most unique book of the Bible. Between the laborious detail and what seemed to be a droning of repetition and specification, I normally clocked out by the fifth or sixth chapter. O great man of faith that I am! Until one day not so long ago when the Lord showed me that all that droning and repetitious activity that used to put me to sleep reading is, in fact, the point.

The laborious detail, meticulous specifications, and droning repetition are all examples of God showing his children in the desert that he is about the detailed business of doing something that *only he can do*. God desires to be among his people and, in so doing, he sets out singularly to make that happen. The detail shows that God is pursuing two tracks of reality at the same time. On one track, the minutia pictures the utter *impossibility* of entering into his holy presence. So he has to install all these rote methods and provisions designed to reveal the abundance of natural effort required to mitigate that impossibility.

On the other track, and at the same time, Yahweh is demonstrating through *the same detail* his relentless desire to be with his chosen people. By the way, not because of his neediness, but for our desperation. This requires all the particulars to show how impossible the entire transaction is because of the chasm between divine holiness and human sin. Yet to do so God must put down very strict safeguards for the access and interactions in which his children will be blessed to participate, because not even a shadow of sin can be in the presence of God without great provision and atonement.

The arduous detail in the book of Leviticus contrasts God's holiness and the people's sin-stained lives with the incredible and detailed provisions that *he* makes to secure the access. The more detail that has to be exacted with precision, the more he is telling them there is no way they can have access to him unless these incredible lengths are taken.

This is what sin has done. Because of the extreme nature of sin, a very great deal is involved in making access to God's holiness possible. Sin is not tolerated in the presence of God's infinite purity and holiness. This is something Aaron and his sons knew very well. They went through the daily grind of implementing so much detail in their work that it signified to the people over and over that it is impossible for us to get to God. And yet the detail God commands reveals how much he is coming to be our God in spite of our sin.

The requirement for holiness still exists, though, because to tolerate anything less would mean that the Lord violates his own absolute standard. He is not like his human creation—thank God! He is not like a human judge, who may rule according to whim and preference. He is sovereign and he can do anything he desires, but he will not violate his own standard of perfection in holiness, as this is the essence of who he is.

The children of Israel never could have approached God because of the chasm between his holiness and their sin. So in a real sense he made the provision possible by showing them how exceedingly sinful their sin really was, and that they were wholly unable to do anything about it outside of God's initiation.

The laborious details regarding cleansings, sacrifices, and everything else reminds Israel how impossible it is to come to God without his making it happen. All of the detail pictures how much God desires to be with them and why sin has made that such a daily task. They have no way to God except that God provides it. The egregious nature of their sin is so appalling in the presence of the holy God that every day, by every detailed ritual and sacrifice and cleanup duty, they are reminded about what lengths God is willing to go to.

Today, how stunning it is to ponder once again the enormity of what was achieved by Jesus on the cross when we consider the message of Leviticus. Aaron and his sons and their sons after them for generations worked with detailed precision, pinpoint accuracy, and specification (if not, they were dead) as a daily and generational reminder of the impossibility that sin had brought on them to be reconciled with God.

All those generations, all those sacrifices, all the infinite detail, in one holy convergence was, at the appointed time, brought to fruition and completion in Jesus, the one perfect sacrifice. The holiness and justice quotient of God has not changed in the twenty-first century. Its demands related to us are evermore required, while we remain evermore futile in our ability to satisfy those demands by any form or ritual or by any merit.

But we have a bigger problem yet. In the postmodern church, many times the order of merit gets flipped and we end up with an overinflated opinion of our own status in the world, which includes a man-centered salvation for which we cannot pay. Yet the bill has come due.

The View of Man

The unregenerate person is lost, with absolutely no ability on his or her own part to incorporate wits, talents, or negotiating skills to alter that fact.

The status of man cannot be changed by therapy, personal growth, or any of the plethora of self-help materials disguising themselves as Christian resources in bookstores. Some of the postmodern views of man, like those on a postcard, have an element of truth, so there is a self-consoling factor in considering that even a fallen person can do some very good things in life, and that altruistic aims, religious acts of charity, and philanthropic deeds can and do add value to a society. They just cannot lead to salvation.

The following is the counterbalance to the predominant view of man in general, as well as the view held by many in the postmodern church. We pick up our description with man in his natural state. And remember, my use of "man" is neither gender-specific nor age-specific.

Let us introduce a postmodern regular good guy ... Sid. Our Sid is a great guy, but he has gone through life not really believing in a biblical Jesus. He does claim a soft belief in God, but, like many of his friends, Sid thinks that as long as you are doing good that that is what matters, regardless of whether you bring God into the mix. Sid's motto is "God, whoever he is, just expects us to do good, not judge others, and be happy."

This is Sid's best day.

He is cleaned up, shined, and coiffed, having just spent the morning walking two old ladies across the street, rescuing a cat from a burning warehouse, and single-handedly putting out the warehouse fire, after which he spoke at a Rotary breakfast. He did all this before clocking in at eight in the morning at his job. He goes to lunch with the mayor and gets a key to the city for all his morning heroics. On the way home that evening, he gives a performance that tops what he did earlier that day.

Yet the Bible says that without trusting in Christ for his redemption, despite his best deeds on his best day, our good Sid is autonomous, self-willed, a suppressor of the truth, a God-denier, completely depraved, a reprobate, spiritually dead, a hater of God, an enemy of God, a lover of self, a fugitive from God, unable to know the thoughts of God, unable to accept the things of God, a liar, unrighteous, hopeless, helpless, prideful, a recipient of God's wrath, and bound for hell. In short, Sid is a sinner (Rom. 3:23; Prov. 14:12; Rom. 1:18; Isa. 48:4; 1 Tim. 3:5; Rom. 1:28;

Eph. 2:1; James 4:4; 2 Cor. 2:14–15; Rom. 5:6; Eph. 2:2; Rom. 2:5; Rev. 20: 11–15). If you find yourself disquieted by this list, the good news is that it's mercifully over, because I know I left some out. The bad news is … I know I left some out.

Of course the sum of those facts is not good, but the knowledge that they are true is indeed good. But, Sid must be told these facts. The knowledge of the biblical truth of natural man (unrighteous man) challenges the status of a postmodern man-centered view (self-righteous) and forms the beginning of wisdom.

In highlighting the holiness of God, we highlight the not-so-holiness of man. Sid is able to do some good things. But the importance of that pales in contrast to the fact that he is spiritually dead, despite those good things that he does. His problem is sin.

The Problem: A Focused View of Sin

There has never been a word that so accurately defines the essence of the famous quote "Familiarity breeds contempt." To the extent it is still used in church culture, the word *sin* has been dumbed down, minimized, mitigated, scattered, smothered, covered, and served over-easy.

It is called everything from an affliction to a sickness, from a weakness to a problem, from a hindrance to that which can be committed and omitted. I have heard sin described by some in the church as "no big deal" if we ask forgiveness, and sadly I have at times treated it with a similar status in my own life as a believer. I heard one pastor describe sin as "refusing to believe how much God loves you." It is also popularly described by many today as "what keeps you from having the life God wants for you." That is a slight understatement, even by Joel Osteen proportions.

The most common word used for *sin* in the New Testament (Greek: *hamartia*) means "to miss the mark or target." However, the grave and insidious nature of sin, in causing us to miss the mark, gets understated. The truth is that sin is missing the mark by galactic dimensions.

In scope and ramifications, it is like being in a room, throwing darts at a board from twenty feet away, and missing the center bull's-eye. But you not only miss the bull's-eye, you miss the entire board, the wall to which the board is connected, the building that contains the wall, the street the building is on, the town, county, state, and country, the planet housed by the solar system, and the solar system that is housed by the universe. This is the aspect of sin as measured in dimension and scale regarding how far from the target of righteousness we have actually missed. And we have galaxies far, far away yet to go!

God says that our sins separate us from him: "Behold, the LORD's hand is not shortened, that it cannot save; nor His ear heavy, that it cannot hear. But your iniquities have separated you from your God; and your sins have hidden His face from you, so that He will not hear" (Isa. 59:1–2). That means there is broken communication—broken fellowship.

Sin is the transgressing or breaking of the laws and commandments of God. That status catapults good Sid into open rebellion against God. Because, remember, it is God to whom Sid's sin is directed. While Sid resides there in rebellion, he is utterly filthy before God, with nothing but sewer rags to put on top of that filth. As Isaiah put it, "We are all like an unclean thing, and all our righteousnesses are like filthy rags; we all fade as a leaf, and our iniquities, like the wind, have taken us away" (64:6). Sid is a slave in his own unbreakable bonds. Paul said, "For I know that in me (that is, in my flesh) nothing good dwells; for to will is present with me, but how to perform what is good I do not find. For the good that I will to do, I do not do; but the evil I will not to do, that I practice" (Rom. 7:18–19).

At the same time, Sid earns the status of being "self-righteous," having no inclination to seek God or to do any good outside the narrow focus of his self-interest. The Bible teaches that "There is none righteous, no, not one; there is none who understands; there is none who seeks after God. They have all turned aside; they have together become unprofitable; there is none who does good, no, not one" (Rom. 6:23). Sin is literally going to kill Sid.

That is when the real problems begin and real payment becomes due.

As if living in sin as an unbeliever was not bad enough for Sid, there is the added dilemma of his not having any way out of his predicament upon his death. We have reviewed the fact that he is a sinner by virtue of the unrighteousness that defines human nature through the breaking of God's laws. The problem is irresolvable upon his untimely expiration.

One more profound fact to further complicate things is that upon his death, Sid will stand before a just and holy God to plead his case. And God is not like any other judge who can be bribed or bought, or who will decide issues based upon a whim, a hunch, or irritation. He is perfect in his judgments and he is just—another of his unfathomable attributes.

Some More Really Bad News

"Sid, I gotta tell you, we still have some very bad news."

As a vile sinner, who all the while has been squawking about how good he really is, Sid will incur the full wrath (holy recompense) of God, which is specifically designated for a depraved person. "For the wrath of God is revealed from heaven against all ungodliness and unrighteousness of men, who suppress the truth in unrighteousness" (Rom. 1:18). And the last act of that wrath of God finds Sid beginning the first day of the rest of eternity in the Devil's hell, where his payment for sin cannot be satisfied and where words cannot describe the depression and torment of the soul who is forever without God.

George Whitefield, the eighteenth-century preacher, said it as only he could: "But if the bare mentioning of the torments of the damned is so shocking, how terrible must the enduring of them be!"

God's judgment is looming. The scales of that justice are perfectly balanced so that all things are measured by the standard of his perfection in holiness. There is no other standard, for it is a standard of absolute perfection as he is absolutely perfect. Only such perfection begets perfect justice, which cannot be swayed by mitigating circumstances or by ardent plea.

If God judged any other way, he himself could not be perfectly just, because he would violate his own standard of perfection. Sid's sentence will be swift and complete. Any appeal to the bench regarding any good thing he did while alive can only be considered and judged if he then did *everything* perfectly good while alive. That is the standard, and that is the problem. It is very grim news indeed.

The Solution is the Good News

Now, and only now, are we able to joyously see why the gospel is, in fact, good news! Quite simply, there can be good news only to the extent that we are fully acquainted with the fact that there is very, very bad news. By virtue of proclaiming the truth of the Bible, we are giving a more complete and accurate picture of truth to keep us from building our lives on a postcard version of the truth, and to help us see the entirety of the truth as detailed by Scripture.

As the problem has been stated, man is fallen in his sin, separated by God with no prospect of return. So Sid has broken the commandments of God, and when he stands before the Creator in judgment, he will be required to pay for his deeds. The problem is that he *cannot* pay. To be clear, Sid's sins must incur the righteous and holy anger (wrath) of God upon them, which God was pleased to transfer to Jesus on the cross—if Sid accepts the transaction.

Jesus bore the wrath of the Father and the humiliation of a cross to redeem in full payment all who would be saved. And that wrath is a holy anger. It is not petty, like when we become angry. It is a holy payment for breaking God's holy law. If Sid recognizes the goodness of God by repenting and turning from his sin, and if he trusts (has faith in) Jesus to save him through the grace of God, then this marvelous exchange takes place.

Everything that is unrighteous about Sid's former nature is taken by Jesus on the cross, and all of Jesus' goodness (righteousness) is then accounted to Sid (Rom. 2:4; 5:12–21; Eph. 2:8; Mark 1:15). Sid is then declared by God to be righteous (justified), as decreed by heaven and based upon the blood sacrifice and resurrection of Jesus.

The act of that justification does not just legally pardon him. For to be only pardoned means that the judge annuls the charge while the crime is still out there to be known and talked about. Some crook got a pardon, but everyone in town knows he is still a crook. Charles Lieter speaks brilliantly of this in his book *Justification and Regeneration*. He says that God, by his justification of the believer through Jesus Christ, wipes the slate clean as if the crime or even the charge had never been transacted.

The believer goes free entirely on the basis of the work done by Jesus through his sacrificial death on the cross. God decrees that act as both sufficient and complete. Then the Holy Spirit comes and leads Sid's daily work of being set apart in holiness (sanctification) and living his life in glorifying God in the earth. When there are times that he does struggle with sin, Sid repents and asks the Holy Spirit for the grace and power to continue on the journey, and on he goes.

When Sid dies and stands before God at the judgment, he will receive his full inheritance of eternal life and reward because the payment for sin has been secured by Jesus' atonement through his blood poured out from a sinless life of perfection. Sid is saved, forever with a good God, and that is the good news of the gospel.

God's directive for evangelism is clear—we must share the true gospel.

We are compelled by the Lord to tell people who he is, who man is, and all about the scourge of sin. We must tell sinners that they are required to repent—to forsake their sin with a proactive change of heart and action—and that fruit of repentance will become evident in the life of the believer. Jesus said to the prostitute, "Go and sin no more."

Repentance and forgiveness do not imply that we will never sin again. They simply mean we are no longer bound by the practice of sin that has held us in bondage, because we have submitted ourselves to the sanctification of the Holy Spirit. So when we do sin, as we certainly will, repentance becomes the heavenly grace that produces the godly sorrow for which we are able to receive the forgiveness that is granted by the goodness of God.

The concept of repentance is repugnant to the postmodern culture because it implies acknowledging and owning sin and guilt and the need for a Savior to do for us what we are unable to do for ourselves in being made righteous before a holy God.

That is all the more reason that the grace of repentance must be proclaimed. It is a true, purely refined treasury of gold.

Repentance: A Treasury of Grace

I HAVE ALREADY shared how God blessed my life in the fall of 2008 when I was brought to focus on the concept of repentance. I want to expand on a broader and deeper scale on this incredible doctrine and to understand it in its rightful position in the economy of God and his church.

The postmodern church, as a matter of practice and on the whole, has deemphasized the doctrine of repentance. And I mean biblical repentance, because its very nature is not particularly market-driven in emphasis, nor is its practice especially warm and fuzzy. In fact, like much of the gospel, true repentance requires a posture that is not usually flattering because it requires self-examination, ownership, brokenness, and, when appropriate, restitution.

The incorporation of its practice as a pursuit is probably not what you would want to suggest for a hot topic at the Q&A debriefing session of the church growth seminar. It is probably right at the top of the list—along with sin, judgment, the cross, and hell—of topics that should be discussed only in the light of "new conversations" about their old meanings, or whether or not the old assumptions concerning their place and meaning are even necessary now.

When have you last heard an expository message or sermon series on the topics of repentance, judgment, or hell? If you can answer that affirmatively, praise the Lord! If not, why do these doctrines find a reluctant base from which they are proclaimed, in light of the message of the Bible regarding repentance and the emphasis Jesus placed upon its preaching and teaching?

How about a one-question quiz? What was the subject of the first message Jesus preached in the very beginning of his public ministry? (I'll give you a hint: it was not "felt needs" or "friendship evangelism.") According to the Gospel of Mark, Jesus came to Galilee and began to preach, saying, "The time is fulfilled, and the kingdom of God is at hand. Repent, and believe in the gospel" (Mark 1:15).

This is recorded as the first public sermon of Jesus according to Matthew's gospel as well. Matthew records the event as being after Jesus comes out of the wilderness temptation with the Devil and, just as Mark records, Matthew's version finds the Lord heading to Galilee to begin his ministry: "From that time Jesus began to preach and to say, "Repent, for the kingdom of heaven is at hand" (Matt. 4:17).

The message of repentance was the first one Jesus preached, and it is no stretch to think Jesus began with his most important message. Is it just possible to assume that Jesus, among other kingdom purposes, was laying a cornerstone and setting a precedent for revealing the significance of repentance that would retain a thread throughout his entire ministry over the next three years?

John the Baptist, whose message was exclusively repentance for the forgiveness of sins, also magnified the message because of his role as a forerunner to the Messiah, in making way for Jesus. It is no surprise that the commonality of both their messages was the theme of repentance.

Jesus, in response to the derision of the Pharisees (as recorded in the sixteenth chapter of Luke), reminded them that their way to justification by "the Law and the Prophets" was no longer valid since John had announced that repentance and belief were the means to their salvation. The law was not abolished; rather it was fulfilled in Jesus.

What Jesus first preached was not only initially important, but was important throughout his entire ministry. And in this message he establishes that repentance is indeed a foundational truth of the gospel message. The theme of repentance was emphasized and repeated over and over in Luke's gospel. Jesus says "I have not come to call the righteous, but sinners, to repentance" (Luke 5:32).

In the thirteenth chapter of Luke we find people having a conversation with Jesus about Pilate putting to death some Galileans who had apparently crossed legal lines of worship acceptable to Roman standards. As was the case in Jewish tradition, many held to the notion that untimely and tragic deaths were the product of sin, and there was quite a buzz apparently as the news become known. Jesus answers them by saying, "Do you suppose that these Galileans were worse sinners that all other Galileans, because they suffered such things? I tell you, no; but unless you *repent, you will all likewise perish*" (Luke 13:2–3, emphasis mine).

In the very next passage Jesus comments on the tragedy of some workers being killed in an accident in Siloam. Again, he rebuffs speculation that this happened as retribution for their guilt, and he uses the situation to discuss the state of those who do not repent: "but unless you *repent,* you will likewise perish" (Luke 13:5, emphasis mine).

Speaking to his disciples just before his ascension, Jesus says, "that *repentance and remission of sins should be preached* in His name to all nations, beginning at Jerusalem" (Luke 24:47, emphasis mine).

A Prodigal Son Returns Home

But perhaps the definitive example in the Gospels highlighting the grace of repentance and its redemptive role in life is found in an entire parable that Jesus teaches in Luke chapter 15. We know it as the parable of the prodigal son. Repentance is one of two very predominant themes in this parable. The first is that of a loving, gracious forgiving father, who is pictured running with open arms to a returning wayward son. It is an amazing image showing us how incredibly good and merciful our heavenly Father is, as well as how willing he is to restore what was lost.

The second theme is an insight into both the inward process and outward fruit of repentance. The word used in the Greek text is *metanoeo*, which means to change one's mind. The idea being that changes in mind will change attitudes and behavior (sin), which in turn gives evidence that the mind *has indeed been changed*. Jesus expands our understanding of this process by describing what repentance is actually creating in this young man—an entirely changed life!

You know the story. The young man runs out of money and has gotten kicked out of every bar on the strip by now. So he just resigns himself to blending in as a "regular Joe" in whatever faraway region he was trapped in. He is broke, tired, hungry, and a long way from home. He comes to the place where he thinks about the goodness of his father, and it is here that he begins considering and owning the futility and sinfulness of what he has done. He says to himself, "I will arise and go to my father, and will say to him, 'Father, I have sinned against heaven and before you, and I am no longer worthy to be called your son. Make me like one of your hired servants'" (Luke 15:18–19).

Here we see what makes repentance such a powerful grace in our lives. Notice the sequence. His assessment of the situation brings him to own his sin by virtue of *coming to himself* in verse 17: "But when he came to himself, he said, 'How many of my father's hired servants have bread enough and to spare, and I perish with hunger!'" (5:17). This was the moment when he considered the weight of his sin and the realization of his sinfulness was owned up to.

Secondly, he declares to himself, "I will arise ... and *I will say to him*, Father, I have sinned against heaven and before you" (5:18, emphasis mine). Here we see that part of the inward process of repentance is forming a sorrow for sin, with the confession of sin beginning to form the outward fruit.

It was also formed by the young man's willingness to do anything to regain even minimal favor (as one of the hired servants). The young man may have been wearing filthy, tattered rags by this time, but he had begun to gird himself in the true humility of repentance, in exchange for the gross humiliation and hardening of a life of sin. This inward process is the change of heart that then precipitates an outward change of action and behavior.

In verse 20, Jesus says that "he arose and came to his father." He entered the embrace of his dad's arms a changed man.

I recommend that you read two works that retain the highest accolades on the subject of repentance. The first is *Nature of Repentance* by seventeenth-century Puritan preacher Thomas Watson. The second is a book by eighteenth-century Scottish preacher Thomas Boston titled *Repentance*. They are both amazing works on the subject of repentance and have been indispensible resources in my own journey.

Repentance is a sweet grace that brings restoration and liberty to the soul. Its benefits are too numerous to mention, and at the end of its path is always a deeper and abiding sense of the love and acceptance of God in one's life. It is also required for our salvation. Unfortunately, as a common doctrine, its importance has seemingly been minimized as a matter of church practice.

Repentance—Check the Electrical Closet

At every church and ministry facility for which I have worked over the years, I have noticed that there is always one thing you can count on: The electrical closet becomes the dumping ground for things that do not quite qualify yet for the dumpster but have worn out any recognizable or redeemable practical use. You know the gig—you open the closet door only to find a box of one hundred custom Y2K calendars, showing you how to survive month by month. You are also likely to find a fifty-gallon plastic trash bag of broken Christmas decorations. And finally, no electrical closet would be complete without a folding table to keep it company and get in your way.

Which begs the question, "Why are you in there anyway?"

Electrical closets just seem to inspire creativity in the art of refuse collection, as well as providing inspiration for humans to show their natural proclivities toward rebellion. And it does not matter if the electrical closet is on the first floor or the second floor, or both. I cannot explain why this phenomenon is true, but it is, and I wonder if it extends to any other entities besides churches. Maybe it is just human nature to read "Electrical Closet, No Storage" and reflexively ignore the instruction. Perhaps the perpetrators justify their indifference because they believe the junk they are throwing inside the closet is beyond useless and there are some things even a dumpster will not take.

I can recall a very specific instance when a staff member once told me she had put something in the closet some time back. "I just threw it in there temporarily till I could get it somewhere else," she said. That was in response to the time I found a Herman Munster lunchbox, circa 1966, with someone's 1966 lunch still in it.

Similarly, I find myself wondering if the doctrine of repentance has been tucked away on a shelf in some out-of-the-way closet or back-of-the-property shed—or worse, just not particularly thought about.

Biblical repentance is a foundational doctrine that is basic to Christianity. It runs through the entire fabric of the church through all of its history. In the postmodern church it seems to be absent from a teaching and preaching emphasis—and absent from a form of grace that is readily embraced and corporately practiced.

We have to find which closet it has been put in so we can pull it out, dust it off, and proclaim its merits. We have a generation of people in the church who are ignorant of its meaning and its bountiful benefits because it is hardly ever emphasized. How can we talk about the salvation of people without explaining repentance's role and requirement in that very act of saving someone? It has to be more than a bare mention of its name as a pass-through on our way to the salvation prayer. You will hear it in the abstract or generic reference, maybe, but how will people know what is actually required if they are not told what it is?

Repentance needs to be let out of the closet. It cannot be kept there because of past abuses where people have been the victim of man-made legalistic forms. True biblical repentance cannot be contrived, feigned, improvised, or manufactured; it can only sought and received. If only we would welcome its grace and embrace its benefits, it would be sought as gold.

And repentance needs to be placed before God as an urgent prayer for a visitation and habitation of his grace. It is a grace of God that is sought by the sinner, bought by the blood of Jesus, and brought by the loving conviction of the Holy Spirit, who applies it like a warm salve on a cold, frostbitten wound. It has been MIA long enough in the church and in the lives of its believers. I cannot sufficiently describe its supernatural ability to change the heart, mind, and actions of the one who is blessed to receive its grace.

Repentance is a Grace

We are talking about repentance in really two applications. The first is what happens at conversion. Surely brokenness must accompany a heart that has been awakened to sin and grievous offense toward God, and the soul's taste of sorrow must be evident, though not completed in the convert, even as salvation is made complete. Following perceptually 2 Corinthians 7:11 ("For observe this very thing, that you sorrowed in a godly manner: What diligence it produced in you, what clearing of yourselves, what indignation, what fear, what vehement desire, what zeal, what vindication! In all things you proved yourselves to be clear in this matter"), Whitefield called this "repentance unto salvation." Wesley similarly called it "repentance unto life." At its core there is at least a posture of brokenness, sorrow, and abhorrence of sin that the will and mind be changed, even if it is not an accounting for every individual offense. We do not have to be completed in repentance to be completed in our salvation. Thank God!

The second application is the ongoing grace of repentance available to the believer as he or she goes through life. And it is a grace—an incredible grace. It is our "confession" of our sin and the advocacy of Jesus that cleanses us. Yet the confession as a believer still involves an ownership, brokenness, contrition, and hatred of the sin.

In my blissful ignorance and indifference prior to September 2008, I would not have thought that deep levels of repentance regarding my view of God would be at the top of my most urgent needs in twenty-five years of ministry. I knew I had plenty of problems, mind you; just not thinking that a sinful view of God would be counted among them. By the end of March 2009, suffice to say, my mind was significantly changed concerning the matter.

Repentance is a grace that comes from preaching truths from God's Word concerning it. My heart was pounded in response to preaching I heard on repentance. I had no prior clue that it needed to be, except in the abstract. Additionally, repentance as a grace has been absent from much of the postmodern church because we have lost sight of whom we have offended. David puts it this way: "For I acknowledge my transgressions, and my sin is always before me. Against You, You only, have I sinned, and done this evil in Your sight—That You may be found just when You speak, and blameless when You judge" (Ps. 51:3–4).

Repentance is the grace response that I must seek because I must never lose sight of the fact that I have perpetrated the offense of sin against my heavenly Father. Everyone and everything else, as it relates to my offense, proceeds in descending order from my priority in offense toward the Almighty.

Clearly, apologies and the tangible steps that may involve any form of restitution are certainly transactions directed at real people. What is *not* being called for or described here is a works-merited repentance—a form brought by the institutions of men. The distinction is as clear as any that would differentiate a "work" from a "work of grace."

This is another key, I am certain, as to why the doctrine of repentance has been largely a no-show in the postmodern church. Because of the human-centered nature of much of our church culture, merged with an overdeveloped sense of self, we find it difficult to consider our motivations for repentance outside of how things affect *me*. That is not repentance; that is damage control. I believe this is true because I have been told so dozens of times in counseling and pastoral settings. If I am successful at making repentance all about "me," or even all about the ones I have hurt, then I may be inclined to be very cautious and deliberate in trying to control circumstances and outcomes that could otherwise be out of my control. That is why we devise rationales for not coming clean in repentance because, "It will hurt her," or "There's too much to lose," or—my personal favorite—"It's all in the past; just move on." If I had a dime for every time I heard that one, I could be writing this book from the hammock in Kona.

But the key to true repentance is, in fact, one that is *true*. People cannot be merely sorry they got caught. That alone cannot be the depth of their sorrow and the breadth of their repentance. Even so, many times this is the basis for what passes for true repentance. It has little or no effect, except as an attempted escape hatch from consequences.

Repentance that is not true does not work because it cannot work. Its work is halted at the gate of a superficial sorrow, never allowing the sinner access into the deep places of the heart where change is made and later made evident in a life that is truly turned around.

Finally, true repentance enjoys very little position in the postmodern church today because there is a giant disconnect between our *perceived* need and the *reality* of our need for true repentance. Mind you, it is needed in the theoretical, generic sense—of course. Everyone would say that. Perhaps it is just that God has not shown us, in our church *specifically*, that he is calling for that *particularly*. But of course we will be open to it if he does—*definitely*. We think?

So with very little fruit that becomes evident in such a venture, the doctrine of repentance goes into the electrical closet, along with many of the other great doctrines of our faith. Because we have these great doctrinal assertions in the closet, many in the postmodern church are having "new discussions" about worn-out doctrines, which have the net effect of challenging the truth claims of those doctrines. Let me encourage you to cry out to God for his magnificent gift—the grace of repentance. Proclaim it as you taste its grace in your own life. Encourage all those in the family of God that true repentance is a treasure, a grace from heaven that abounds to the one who would call on the name of the Lord.

It does not always come the same way or with the same ease. It is a grace of Jesus Christ. It must be sought.

Charles Spurgeon, in one of his incredibly insightful words on repentance, encourages the one who is seeking the grace to repent, but has yet to find it:

> But the way for him to repent is by God's grace to believe, to believe and think on Jesus. If he pictures to himself the wounded bleeding side, the crown of thorns, the tears of anguish—if he takes a vision of all that Christ suffered, I will be bound for it he will turn to Him for repentance. I will stake the reputation I may have in spiritual things upon this—that a man cannot, under God's Holy Spirit, contemplate the Cross without a broken heart.[1]

May the Lord grant us the grace to consider the merits of the cross. It is the crowned destination of God's goodness and mercy. It is the place of the grand exchange—my sin for the righteousness of Christ. It has provided our door to repentance, the evidence of how good God is.

"Or do you show contempt for the riches of his kindness, tolerance and patience, not realizing that *God's kindness leads you toward repentance?*" (Rom. 2:4 NIV, emphasis mine).

Postcard Postscript:
Lunch Under the Bamboo Gods!

MY WIFE AND I recently celebrated our twenty-seventh year of marriage by visiting South Florida. One day while there, we got up early and drove down to one of the Florida Keys to have lunch on the beach at a particular restaurant my wife had in mind. While sitting in the beach cabana restaurant, our toes in the sand and taking in all the beautiful sights, we overheard two ladies in their early to midforties talking about church. They were very cheerful, and when we asked our server how far we were from downtown Key West, where we were thinking of going, the ladies heard our question and proceeded to answer for the server. At that point we began to strike up a conversation with them from about fifteen feet away from where they were sitting.

We never did formally introduce ourselves to one another, but one lady, whom I will call "Peg," described herself as the director of a major ministry within the church, and promptly invited my wife and me to their service. I responded, "That's very kind of you; tell us about your church."

A Postmodern Buffet

Peg smiled broadly, identified the name of her church, and proceeded to tell me and Camille how they open their arms to "transvestites, cross-dressers, the outcasts, the arts crowd," and anyone else who may not be welcome at a regular church. And as she named all those her church welcomed, her tone and pauses indicated that she was watching us for our reaction, looking to see if we were shocked and appalled. Of course, we were not. As if going to church with the groups she mentioned was implicitly worse than going to church with liars, drunkards, adulterers, fornicators, people full of rage, or even "good" people who were upstanding citizens, but headed for hell because they were too prideful to humble themselves and be saved. You know, just the regular sinners—the ones she assumed we thought God discriminates from the ones at her church. The real question is not establishing whether or not we are *all* prolific sinners; the question is, have we been forgiven and saved by putting our trust in Jesus?

I asked Peg, "Does your church share the gospel with the people who come to your services?" She looked at me a bit perplexed and responded, "We show them that God is love—if that's the gospel."

The other lady, whom I will call "Lisa," began to detail the history of her journey from Christian high school years ago, which she described as something she "hated," to her recent visitation and commitment to Peg's church. Lisa went on and on about how she was a renegade in school, highlighting her list of sins and how she detested Christians and others who taught from the Bible. She said she wanted nothing of Christianity until she found what she was looking for at Peg's church a short while back.

I asked Peg, the church leader, about her own life's story. She responded that she was a "happily divorced woman" who had then found the love of her life, and for the past several years had been living with him in blissful harmony. She said (without us asking the question) that the fact they were not married did not matter to God, because "some piece of paper" could not validate any more to them than what they knew they had. God had "created us for one another." By the way, her live-in lover was described by her as an "agnostic," and she said she did not discuss stuff about God with him because she did not want to "stir the pot with theological discussions." Keep in mind, she described herself as the director for an important ministry at a large church. It was at this time that Peg told us she was also a board member of the church as well. It was at this revelation that I began thinking to myself, *Who pastors this place, Bill Maher?*

At this point I asked Peg, "Are you born again, Peg? Have you received salvation?" Without hesitation, as if rehearsed and said a million times before, Peg answered, "I've always been a Christian. God got it right the first time. I don't need to be born again." I asked her about repentance, but she just chuckled and repeated the line that "God got it right the first time. I've always been a Christian."

Before I could ask her about the account of Nicodemus and Jesus in the Gospel of John, Lisa began telling us about a comparative religion course she was currently taking, and how she was "blown away by the humanity of Jesus!" She went on and on about what clothes Jesus would wear, where he would hang out, and how amazingly "hip" he would be if he were here today. After several minutes of listening to this Haight-Ashbury description of Jesus, I finally interrupted Lisa and asked her about the original point of Jesus' humanity and how important it was that he was 100 percent human, and how he could be fully acquainted with our temptation, pain, and grief. Camille and I went on to share about Jesus' divinity and his power and authority given by God to forgive sins. Lisa detoured around that conversation and went back to describing images of Jesus in his cool sandals, fitting in comfortably at South Beach, and appreciating other world religions. At this point, all we needed was the Jefferson Airplane on the house system and we could have re-created the Sumer of Love, circa 1967.

When Lisa ended her conversation, we found out that Peg, our church leader and board member, was a pantheist. According to her, God resides everywhere, including not only in all of nature, but even in the bamboo ceiling we were sitting under. She actually confirmed that God was hanging up there, in the very fiber of the bamboo. I am now thinking, *Why didn't we just take a small boat and have lunch in Cuba?*

As Lisa was about to begin her fourth or fifth lap around her own obvious universalist's track, Camille and I got out of our chairs and walked over to their table. I knew God wanted us to listen, and be very attentive, but it had been an hour and a half, and the conversation became very repetitive and circular, and whatever was formerly my lunch had withered into a tiny ball on my plate. I leaned over and gently told them that we live in a postmodern world where the universal truths of the Bible are being assaulted and personally reinterpreted according to what any individual wants to believe. I told them that Camille and I formed our worldview from the Bible, and its transcendent truths are the only thing that will rightly reveal the true message and ministry of Jesus Christ, who is the only way any of us can get to God because of our sinful condition. I told them I pray that they would seek truth through the revelation of God's Word, the authoritative source of true revelation. Camille talked with them about how important it is to believe in what is true instead of subjectively forming their own basis for claiming whatever they desire to be true. We thanked them for the conversation and invitation, then said our goodbyes. And we headed on our way. It had been a stunning ninety minutes.

While it is Yet Day!

It was very revealing talking with those two precious women. And all joking aside, my heart truly went out to them, and I could not get our lunch encounter off my mind for the rest of our trip. It was as if God had given my wife and me a stark case-in-point postmodern church experience. I still think of those two ladies from time to time, and I do pray for them. I hope they are praying for me.

We are here for this time, and the culture is going to test our goods. I encourage us all to stand in the full armor of Christ and in the grace of a good God. Remember, as followers of Jesus, we are *not* entitled to be offended over everything. If we are faithful Christians, we can all know for sure that we will be called intolerant, rigid, dogmatic, religious, and many other things. And that is by the Christians! Yet know that this postmodern culture's belief systems are jaded and confused, so the opportunities for dispensing the truth claims of the Bible are tremendous. Surely that window of opportunity will begin to narrow, even in America, but the present times, although troubling, are exciting indeed. They are exciting because we get these wonderful opportunities to talk with people about the bamboo gods. About how Jesus *is* God, and how the revelation of him and his mission is found in the timeless truths of Scripture.

I really hope this short little journey has been helpful to you. I hope you are left with a sense of knowing a little bit more about postmodernism and the challenges that its pervasive philosophy presents to Christianity. I also hope I have been able to renew the value of proclaiming truth, without being "preachy" in doing so. And I hope I have communicated the urgency of the hour in terms that accurately describe the hour in which we live.

At the same time, however, I truly believe that God is awakening his bride. I have seen that many are renewing the call to preach the Word of God in an uncompromising proclamation.

In the meantime, as we continue getting those postcards from the postmodern church, let us consult our travel agent—the Holy Spirit—before booking the week's vacation. Then we must read the detailed brochure—the Bible. Only then will we be able to make informed decisions about our destination. From the Word of God we will know where we are going, while finding grace to embrace the journey, even in great trial.

Then we can tell everyone about our trip and about the goodness and saving love of Jesus. Some will listen; most will not. But tell everyone in any case. After all, "How then shall they call on Him in whom they have not believed? And how shall they believe in Him of whom they have not heard? And how shall they hear without a preacher?" (Rom. 10:14).

God is good! May he richly bless and keep you by his faithfulness.

Have a nice trip.

Notes

Chapter 2

1. Brian Ingraffia, *Postmodern Theory and Biblical Theology* (New York, NY: Cambridge Press, 1995), 4.

Chapter 6

1. Andy Crouch, "The Emergent Mystique," *Christianity Today*, November 2004, 36.
2. Rob Bell, *Velvet Elvis* (Grand Rapids, Mich.: Zondervan, 2005), 44.

Chapter 10

1. R. C. Sproul, *The Holiness of God* (Wheaton, Ill.: Tyndale House, 1985), 40.

Chapter 11

1. Charles Spurgeon's sermon "Repentance Unto Life," delivered September 23, 1855, at New Park Chapel, Southwark.